my first book of QUESTIONS AND ANSWERS
about
SCIENCE
AND
NATURE

Rosie Greenwood, Sue Nicholson and Clare Oliver

p

This is a Parragon Book
First published in 2001

Parragon
Queen Street House
4 Queen Street
Bath BA1 1HE, UK

Produced by

David West ⚇ Children's Books
7 Princeton Court
55 Felsham Road
Putney
London SW15 1AZ

British Library Cataloguing-in-Publication
Data

A catalogue record for this book is
available from the British Library.

ISBN 0-75255-842-0

Printed in China

Designers
Axis Design, Aarti Parmar, Rob Shone,
Fiona Thorne

Illustrators
Derek Bazell, Biz Hull, Julie Scott
(Artist Partners)
Gilly Marklew, Janie Perie, Sarah Smith,
Mike Taylor, Ross Watton
(SGA)

Cartoonist
Peter Wilks (SGA)

Editor
James Pickering

CONTENTS

WHERE DO SHADOWS COME FROM? and other questions about simple science

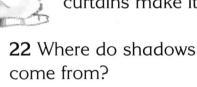

27 How do batteries make electricity?

28 How can I see sound?

29 How do sounds travel along telephone wires?

30 Do magnets have glue in them?

30 How do magnets push and pull?

31 How do magnets help explorers?

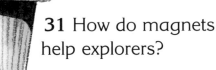

32 Why are slides slippery?

33 Why do bikes have brakes?

34 Why do I fall over?

35 How fast do skydivers fall?

35 What makes things heavy?

WHAT DO MY LUNGS DO?
and other questions about my body

38 Am I special?

38 What am I made of?

39 What can my body do?

40 What's my skin for?

41 Why do my fingers go wrinkly in the bath?

41 Why do some people have freckles?

42 Why do I need haircuts?

43 Why do I get goosebumps?

43 Why is some hair straight and some curly?

44 How many bones do I have?

45 What are bones for?

45 Where is my funny bone?

46 What do muscles do?

47 How do muscles work?

48 Where does my food go?

49 What are teeth for?

49 Why do I go to the toilet?

50 What's blood for?

50 What does my heart do?

51 Where's my heart?

51 Can I feel my heart beating?

52 What do my lungs do?

52 What makes me yawn?

53 What happens when I breathe?

54 What are nerves?

55 Why do I get pins and needles?

55 What does my brain do?

56 How do my eyes help me see?

57 How do my ears help me hear?

58 What's my nose for?

59 Why can't I taste food if I have a cold?

60 What is chickenpox?

61 Why do I sometimes get sick?

61 How do I stay healthy?

62 Where did I come from?

63 What's my tummy button?

64 Why do I sleep?

65 Why do I dream?

65 What's sleepwalking?

WHICH ANIMALS HAVE SCALY SKIN? and other questions about types of animals

68 What do a mosquito and an elephant have in common?

68 Which plant is really an animal?

69 What are the simplest life-forms?

70 Which animals are spineless?

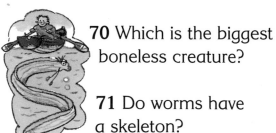

70 Which is the biggest boneless creature?

71 Do worms have a skeleton?

72 What sort of animal is a lobster?

72 Who wears armour at the bottom of the sea?

73 How do crabs grow bigger?

74 Which animals have a skeleton on the outside?

74 Are spiders insects?

75 Can insects fly?

76 How do fish breathe?

76 How do salmon leap?

77 Which fish would fit on your fingertip?

78 Why are frogs slimy?

78 How can you tell a frog from a toad?

79 Which is the weirdest amphibian?

80 Which animals have scaly skin?

80 How long do tortoises live?

81 How can you tell a crocodile from an alligator?

82 Why do birds have feathers?

83 Can all birds swim?

83 Why do eagles have such hooked beaks?

84 Which animals have fur?

84 Are all mammals soft to touch?

85 Which is the tiniest mammal?

86 What type of animal is a koala?

86 Which mammal lays eggs?

87 Do all mammals breathe through the mouth?

88 Which lizard looks like a tree trunk?

88 Why are zebras stripy?

89 Who wears two fur coats?

90 Do turtles lay eggs in the sea?

90 Which bird lays the biggest egg?

91 Do tree frogs lay eggs in trees?

92 Which dad has babies?

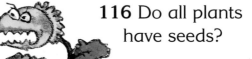

Where do shadows come from?

and other questions about simple science

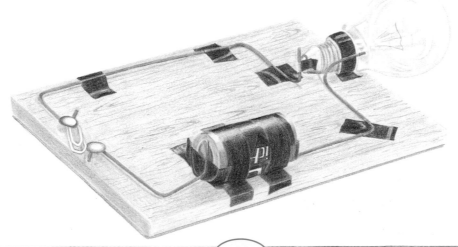

What is air made of?

Air is a mixture of invisible gases. The main ones are nitrogen and oxygen, but there's also some carbon dioxide, water vapour and other gases, as well as tiny bits of salt, dust and dirt.

How do we know air is there?

We can't see or taste or smell air, but we can feel and hear it when the wind blows. Wind is moving air – it's what makes trees bend and leaves rustle, and what blows sailing boats across the water.

❓ *Is there air in Space?*

The skin of air around the Earth is called the atmosphere, and it fades away into nothingness at about 500 km above the ground – that's where Space begins. There's no air in Space, but most of the other planets have their own atmospheres.

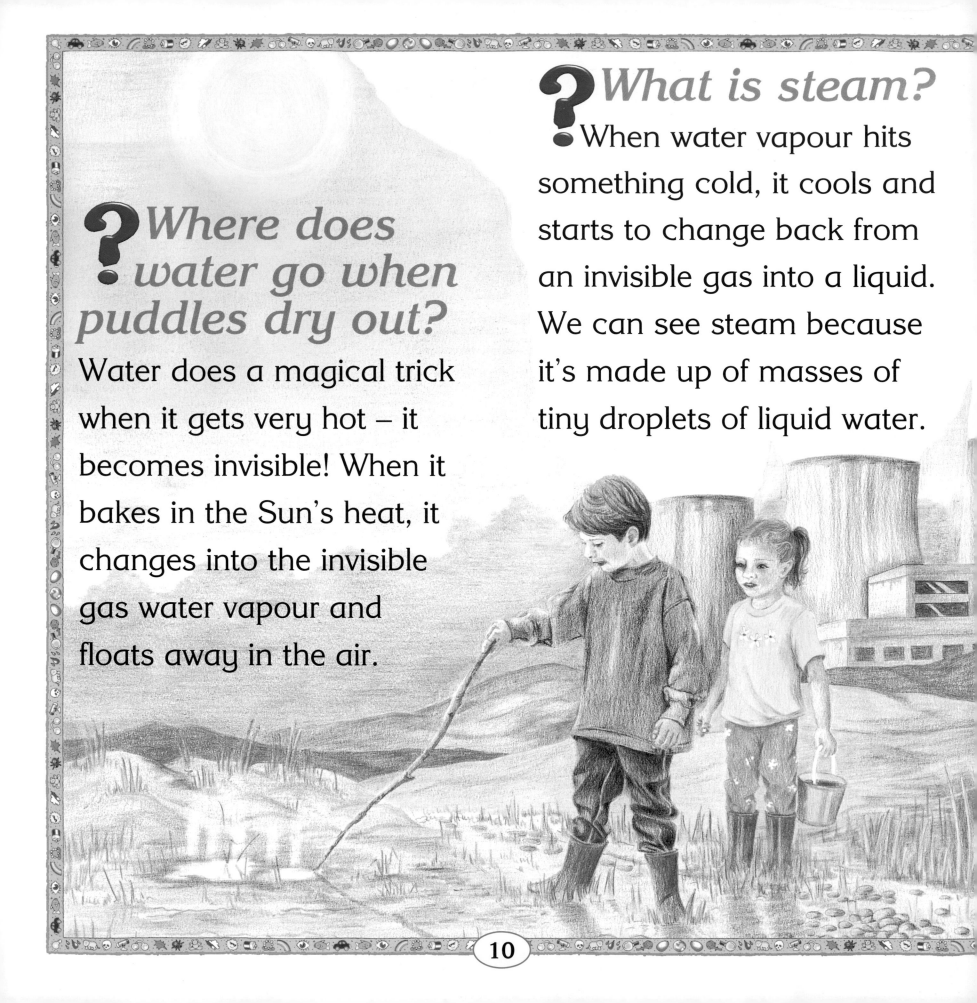

?Where does water go when puddles dry out?

Water does a magical trick when it gets very hot – it becomes invisible! When it bakes in the Sun's heat, it changes into the invisible gas water vapour and floats away in the air.

?What is steam?

When water vapour hits something cold, it cools and starts to change back from an invisible gas into a liquid. We can see steam because it's made up of masses of tiny droplets of liquid water.

? *Where does ice come from?*

Ice is what happens when water gets very, very cold – it freezes into a solid. Most materials will change from a liquid into a gas if they get hot enough, and from a liquid into a solid if they get cold enough.

? *Why do balloons get bigger?*

One reason balloons get bigger is because you're blowing lots of air into them. The other is because they're made of a stretchy material called rubber. But don't forget to tie a knot to hold the air in, or your balloons will shrink again very quickly!

TRUE OR FALSE?

You cannot weigh air.

FALSE. Like everything on Earth, air has weight – 4,000 balloons would weigh the same as a tub of ice cream.

❓ *Why do balloons float?*

Things float upwards when they're lighter than their surroundings. Air-filled balloons are roughly the same weight as the air around them, which is why they don't float all that well. The best floaters are filled with a gas that's much lighter than air. It's called helium, and it's used in airships as well as in party balloons.

Most fish use balloons to help them float.

TRUE. Most fish have a gas-filled bag called a swim bladder inside them, which helps them float.

? Why do rubber ducks float in the bath?

Air is lighter than water, and one reason a rubber duck floats is because it's stuffed full of air. The water helps, too, because it pushes up on the duck. This upwards push is called upthrust.

? Why does the water level rise when I get in the bath?

When you get in the bath, your body pushes the water out of the way. The only place the water can go is up, so the water level rises.

❓*Why does the soap sink?*

Things will float in water only if they are lighter than the amount of water they push aside. If they are heavier, the water's upthrust isn't strong enough to hold them up. A bar of soap will sink if it's heavier than the amount of water it pushes aside.

? *Where does sugar go in hot drinks?*

Sugar doesn't just vanish in hot drinks, it does the same trick in cold ones. It doesn't completely disappear, though – you can taste it's there. You can't see the sugar, because it spreads completely into the water. We call this dissolving.

❓ *Why do fizzy drinks have bubbles?*

The bubbles in fizzy drinks are the gas carbon dioxide. You can't see them when the top is on the bottle because the carbon dioxide is dissolved in the water.

Lots of carbon dioxide is squashed into the drink, and when you open the bottle, the gas escapes as bubbles.

Fish breathe air just as we do.

FALSE. They breathe the oxygen dissolved in water.

Salt comes from sea water.

TRUE. It's dissolved in sea water. To separate it, sea water is heated until the water changes into gas and floats away, leaving the salt behind.

? *Why can't we see in the dark?*

We can't see in the dark because we can't see without light. Objects like trees and houses don't give off their own light, even in the daytime. We can only see them because sunlight is bouncing off them into our eyes. This bouncing off is called reflection.

?Why can I see myself in a mirror?

When light hits something rough like a blanket, it scatters in all directions – like spilling sugar. But when light hits something smooth like a mirror, it comes straight back – like a ball bouncing off a wall. You see yourself in a mirror because light bounces off your face towards the mirror, and then straight back into your eyes.

The Moon shines with its own light.

FALSE. Moonlight is sunshine bouncing off the Moon towards us.

Cats have mirrors in their eyes.

TRUE. Cats' eyes have a mirror-like layer to help them see in the dark.

Sunlight

Raindrop

Light spreads into colours.

? Is light white?

Light may look white sometimes, but it's really a mixture of all the colours of the rainbow – red, orange, yellow, green, blue, indigo (violet-blue), violet.

? Why do rainbows happen?

Rainbows happen when sunlight passes through water drops. The water drops make white light spread into all its colours, and we see a rainbow.

❓*Why is grass green?*

When light hits something, only some of its colours bounce back. Grass looks green because only green light bounces off it – the other colours of light are swallowed up.

Green light bounces off grass.

Sunlight

Grass

TRUE OR FALSE?

You can visit the end of the rainbow.

FALSE. When you move, the rainbow seems to move with you – you always stay in the middle of the rainbow.

Birds can't see colours.

FALSE. Although lots of animals can't see colours, birds can.

? Why does opening the curtains make it light?

Light can pass through some materials, such as window glass, but not others. When materials let light through, we call them transparent.

? Where do shadows come from?

Your body isn't transparent, so it blocks the light and makes the dark patch we call a shadow form. You can test this out on a sunny day – to see your shadow, stand with your back to the Sun.

? Why does drawing the curtains make it dark?

When things don't let light through, we call them opaque. If curtains are made of thick, heavy cloth, they can be opaque enough to block light and make rooms dark, even during the day.

Transparent

Opaque

23

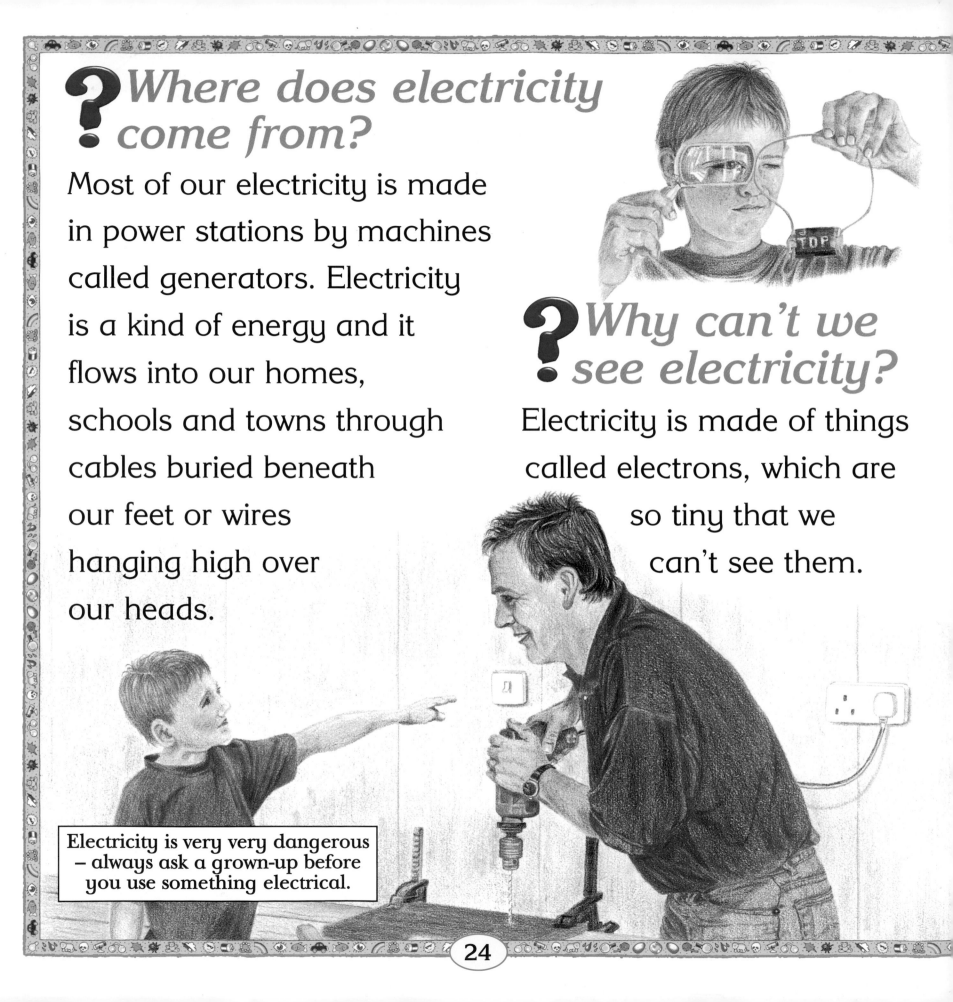

❓ *Where does electricity come from?*

Most of our electricity is made in power stations by machines called generators. Electricity is a kind of energy and it flows into our homes, schools and towns through cables buried beneath our feet or wires hanging high over our heads.

Electricity is very very dangerous – always ask a grown-up before you use something electrical.

❓ *Why can't we see electricity?*

Electricity is made of things called electrons, which are so tiny that we can't see them.

?How can I make electricity?

You can make a safe kind of electricity by rubbing a balloon against a nylon jumper. It's called static electricity and it has pulling power – test this out by sticking the balloon on a wall.

TRUE OR FALSE?

Wind is used to make electricity.

TRUE. Electricity generators are powered by wind, water, coal, oil, gas or nuclear fuel.

Our electricity comes from the sky.

FALSE. Lightning is a flash of static electricity, but it isn't used to power things.

? Why do things stop working when you switch them off?

Electricity only works when it can flow all the way around a loop called a circuit. Turning off a switch breaks the circuit, stopping the flow and turning electrical things like lights off. Turning a switch on joins the circuit and makes them work again.

Ask a grown-up to help you make this simple switch and circuit.

Drawing pin

Paper clips act as a switch.

26

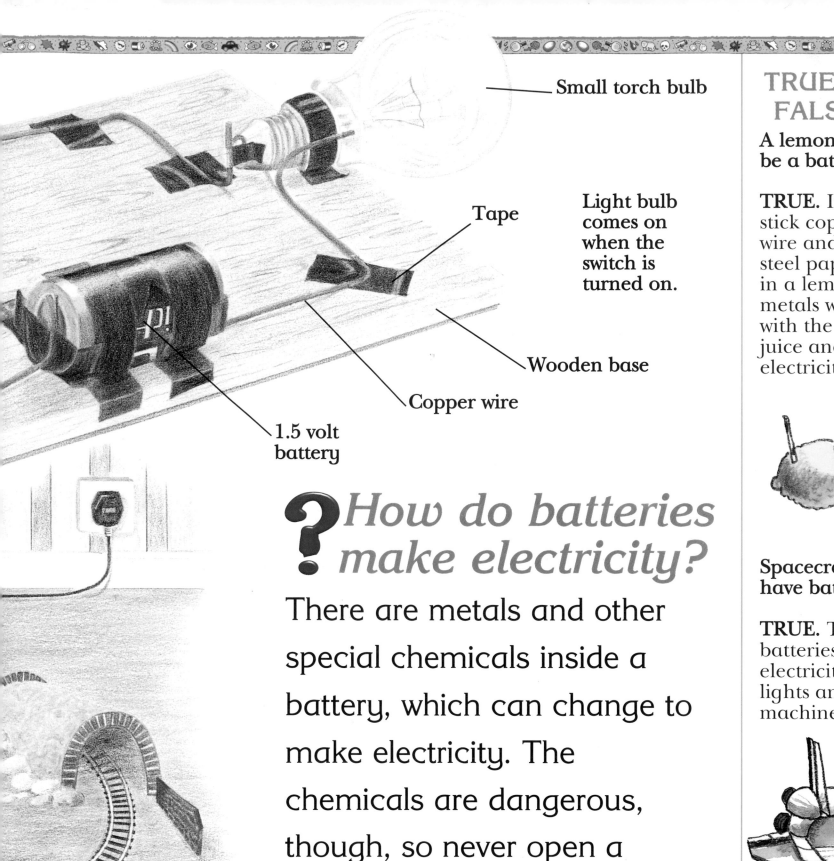

Small torch bulb

Tape

Light bulb comes on when the switch is turned on.

Wooden base

Copper wire

1.5 volt battery

? *How do batteries make electricity?*

There are metals and other special chemicals inside a battery, which can change to make electricity. The chemicals are dangerous, though, so never open a battery to look at them.

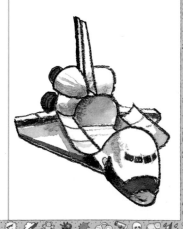

? How can I see sound?

Sound is a kind of energy which happens when something vibrates, or shakes, and makes the air around it vibrate as well. The vibrations travel through the air into your ears, and you hear sounds. You can see sound energy if you sprinkle sugar on a drum and then hit it with a stick. The vibrations will make the sugar shake up and down.

❓ *How do sounds travel along telephone wires?*

Telephones have a microphone in them which changes sound energy into electricity. The electricity flows through wires to another telephone, where a small speaker changes the electricity back into sound energy.

TRUE OR FALSE?

All phones need wires.

FALSE. Mobile phones change sound energy into radio signals, which can travel a long way without wires.

You can't hear sounds underwater.

FALSE. Sounds can travel through water and all sorts of other materials.

? Do magnets have glue in them?

No, magnets work because they have an invisible force called magnetism. Most magnets are made of iron or steel, and their magnetism pulls objects made of iron or steel towards them.

? How do magnets push and pull?

The two ends of a magnet are called its north and south poles. If you have two magnets, the north pole of one will attract (pull) the south pole of the other towards it. Two north poles or two south poles will repel (push) each other away.

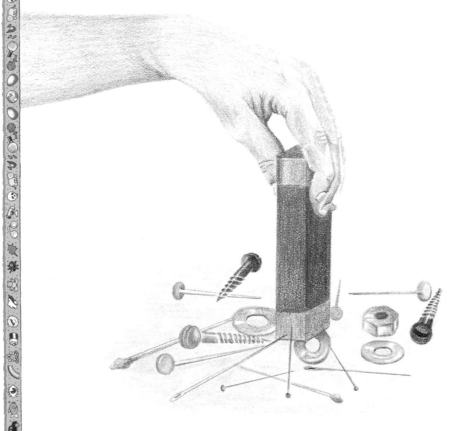

? How do magnets help explorers?

Magnets are used in compasses because if a magnet can move freely, its north pole will always swing round to point towards the Earth's North Pole. You can test this out by hanging a bar magnet on a piece of string.

Magnet lines up with north.

NORTH

TRUE OR FALSE?

The Earth is a magnet.

TRUE. Its south magnetic pole is near the North Pole, and its north magnetic pole is near the South Pole.

Your fingers will stick to a magnet.

FALSE. Only iron or steel objects will stick to a magnet.

31

? Why are slides slippery?

Friction is a slowing force which happens when two surfaces rub against each other. Rough surfaces create stronger friction than smooth ones do, which is why slides are given smooth slippery surfaces. Can you imagine how difficult it would be to slide down a rough concrete ramp?

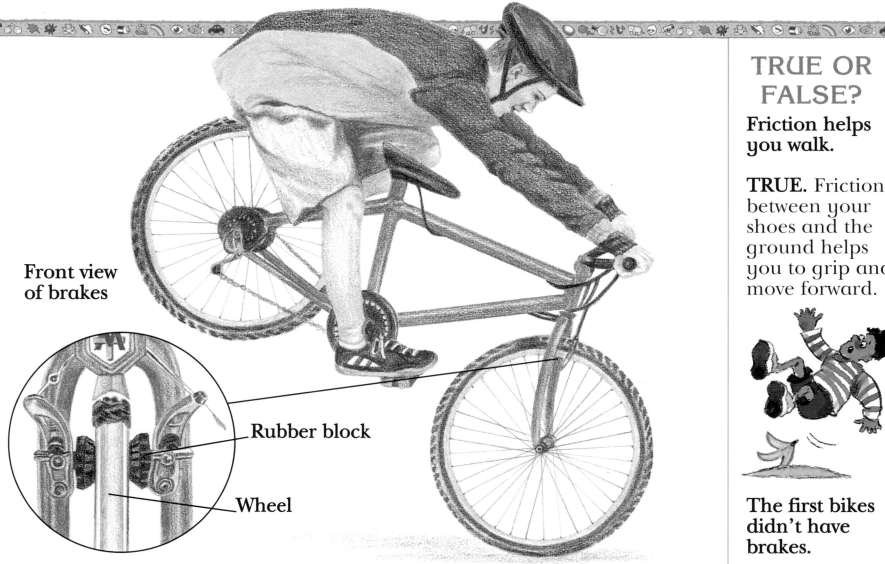

Front view
of brakes

Rubber block

Wheel

?*Why do bikes have brakes?*

Brakes help a bike to stop, of course – but do you know why? It's because brakes use friction. When you squeeze the brakes, rubber blocks press against the wheels. The friction between the blocks and the wheels slows your bike down.

Friction helps you walk.

TRUE. Friction between your shoes and the ground helps you to grip and move forward.

The first bikes didn't have brakes.

TRUE. When the earliest bicycles were made in the 1790s, they didn't have brakes or pedals.

Why do I fall over?

You might start to fall because you trip, but it's the invisible force of gravity that makes you end up on the ground. Gravity is a real downer – it's what tugs everything on Earth towards the ground and stops things like footballs from flying off into Space.

How fast do skydivers fall?

When skydivers jump out of an aeroplane they drop towards the ground at about 190 kph. Opening a parachute slows the skydiver down to about 20 kph – but that's still a lot faster than you can run!

What makes things heavy?

Gravity does! Weight is the effect of gravity on an object's mass – the amount of stuff it's made of. The more mass something has, the more gravity tugs it down and the heavier it is.

What do my lungs do?

and other questions about my body

?Am I special?

?Yes, because there's only one person like you in the whole wide world! We all have different coloured hair, skin and eyes, we may be tall or short and we all walk and talk differently.

What do you look like?

?What am I made of?

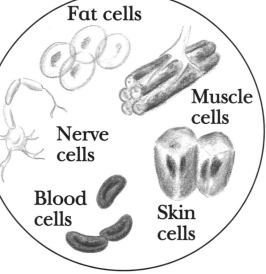

Fat cells

Muscle cells

Nerve cells

Blood cells

Skin cells

Your body is made up of millions of tiny cells. You have lots of different kinds of cells. Each kind has a special job to do. Your cells work together to keep you alive.

What can my body do?

All sorts of amazing things! The different parts of your body – both the outside parts and the inside parts like your heart, bones and muscles that you can't see – all work together so you can laugh, cry, walk, talk, jump, hop, run, think, read and sleep!

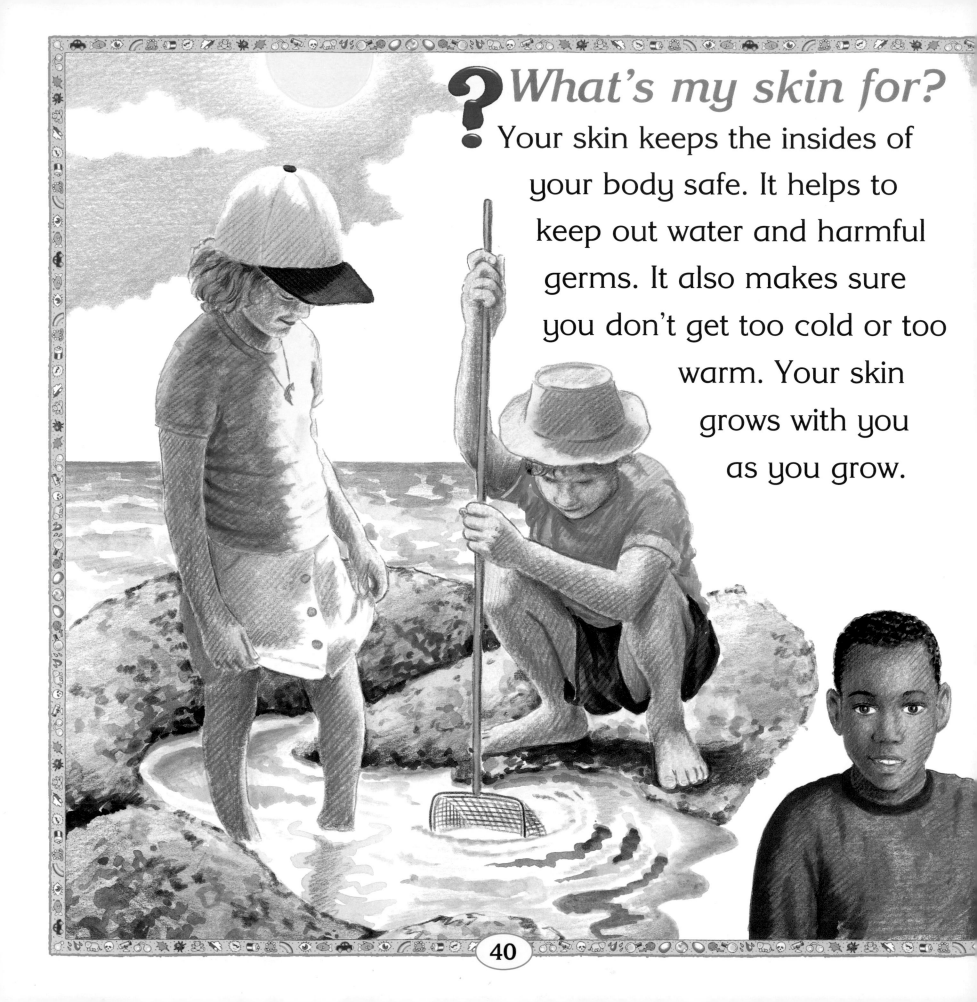

? What's my skin for?

Your skin keeps the insides of your body safe. It helps to keep out water and harmful germs. It also makes sure you don't get too cold or too warm. Your skin grows with you as you grow.

? Why do my fingers go wrinkly in the bath?

Your skin contains oil that helps to make it waterproof, like a raincoat. Fingers and toes don't have this oil, so the ends get wrinkly if you stay in water for a long time.

? Why do some people have freckles?

Skin contains a special colouring called melanin, which protects it from strong sunlight. Freckles are patches of extra melanin, which can appear on fair skin when it has been in the sun. Dark skin has more melanin than pale skin.

❓ *Why do I need haircuts?*

Your hair is always growing, that's why! Hair grows quite slowly though, at about 2 mm every week. It grows a bit faster in the summer than in the winter. Hair is made out of keratin. So are your fingernails and toenails.

? Why do I get goosebumps?

Your whole body is covered with tiny hairs except on the palms of your hands and the soles of your feet. When you get chilly, little muscles in your skin push the hairs up to trap warm air, and you get goosebumps.

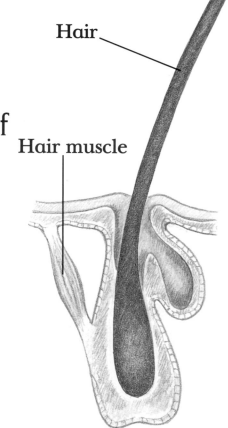

Hair

Hair muscle

? Why is some hair straight and some curly?

Hair grows out of tiny holes in our skin. If the hole is round, then our hair grows straight. If the hole if flat, our hair grows curly.

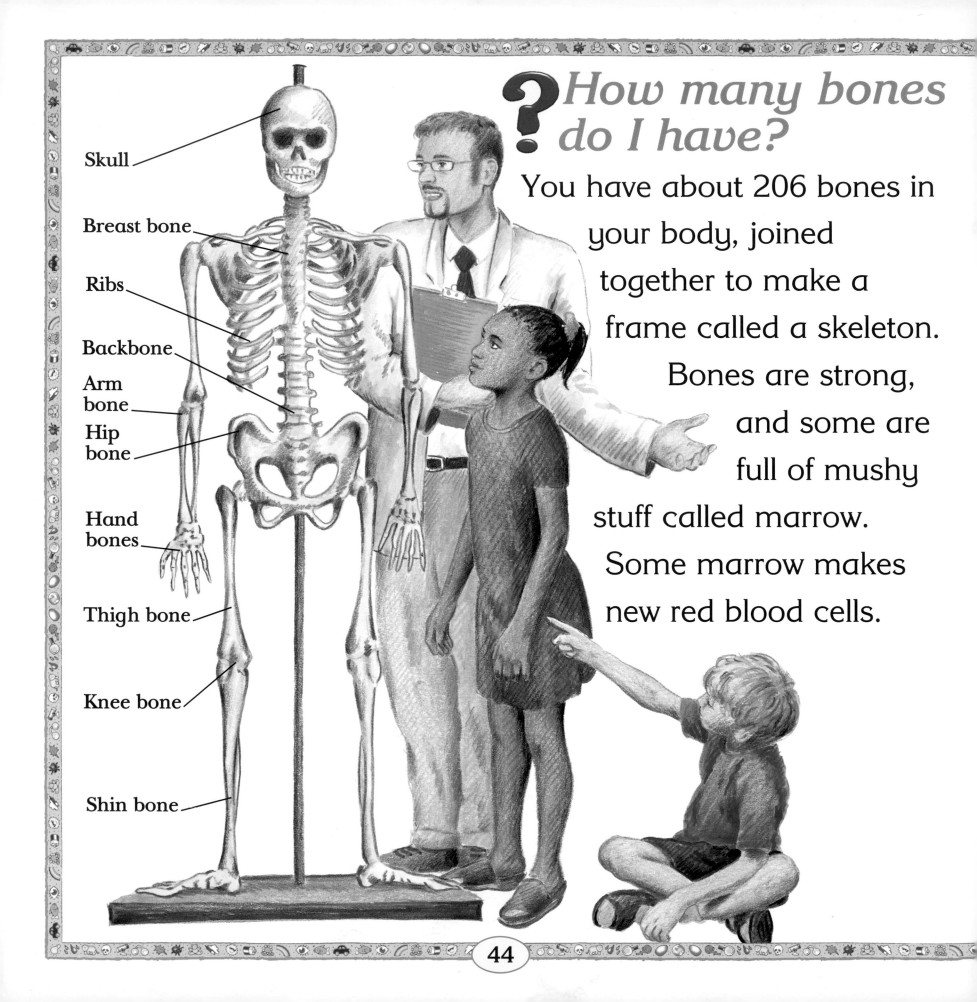

How many bones do I have?

Skull

Breast bone

Ribs

Backbone

Arm bone

Hip bone

Hand bones

Thigh bone

Knee bone

Shin bone

You have about 206 bones in your body, joined together to make a frame called a skeleton. Bones are strong, and some are full of mushy stuff called marrow. Some marrow makes new red blood cells.

? What are bones for?

Bones hold you up. Without them you'd be a floppy jellyfish! Your bones also help to protect the soft parts inside your body – your skull protects your brain, and your ribs protect your heart and lungs. Your bones help you make lots of different movements.

? Where is my funny bone?

Your funny bone is on your elbow. It has a big nerve running over it. If you bang it you may feel a strange tingle that can hurt.

?What do muscles do?

Muscles help you move. Muscles in your arms lift and pull. Muscles in your thumbs help you to hold things. Muscles in your chest help you to breathe. You have more than 600 muscles to help you move different parts of your body.

How do muscles work?

Muscles are fixed to your bones and usually work in pairs. They tighten to pull a bone one way, and loosen to let the bone move back again.

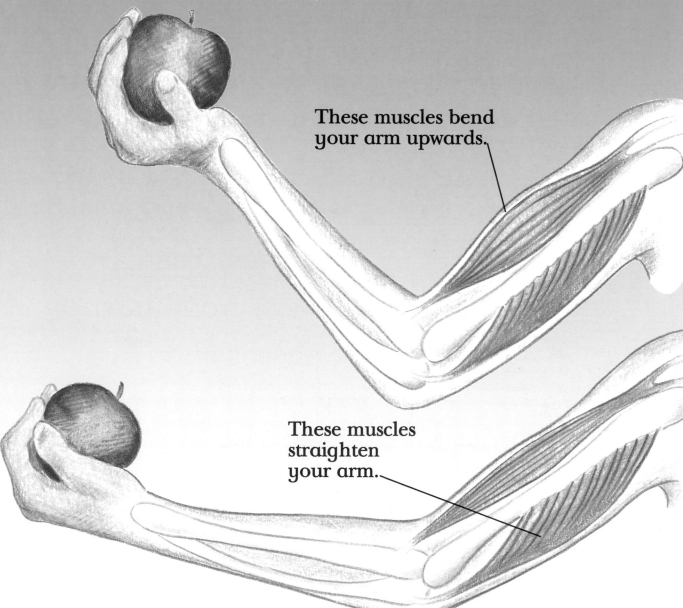

These muscles bend your arm upwards.

These muscles straighten your arm.

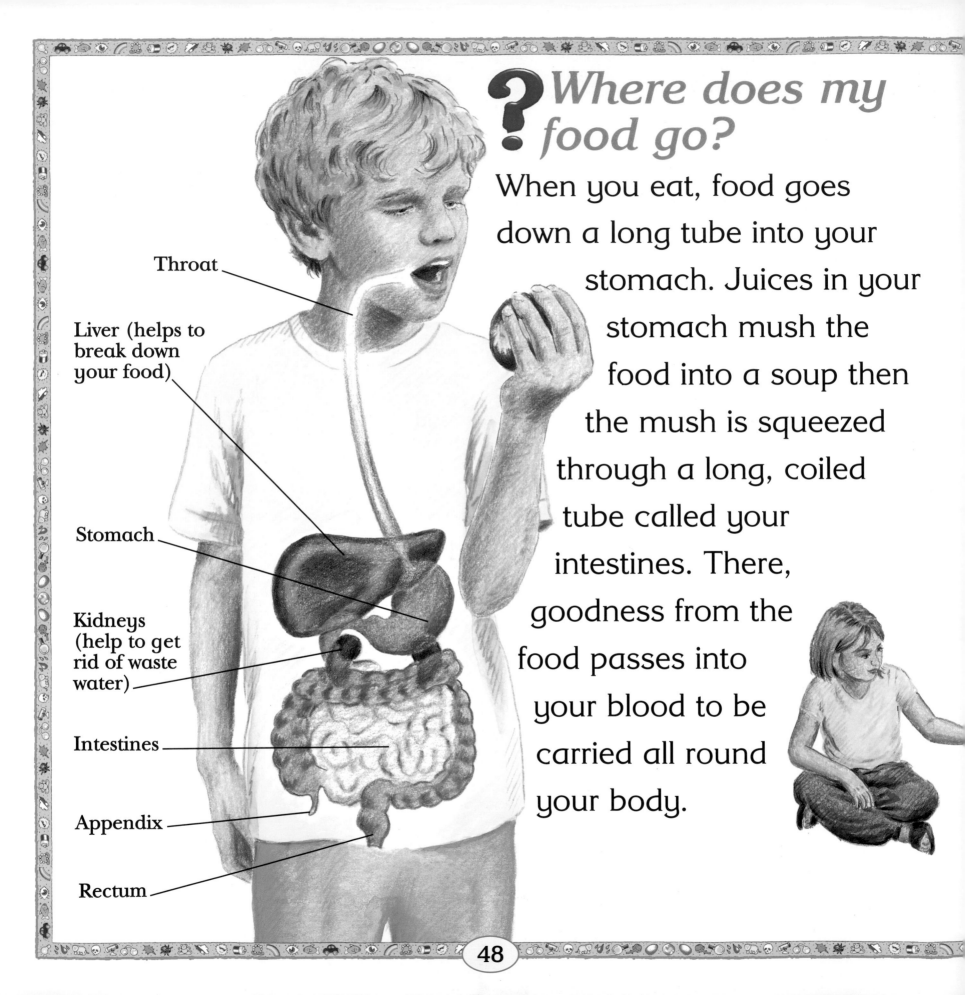

? *Where does my food go?*

Throat

Liver (helps to break down your food)

Stomach

Kidneys (help to get rid of waste water)

Intestines

Appendix

Rectum

When you eat, food goes down a long tube into your stomach. Juices in your stomach mush the food into a soup then the mush is squeezed through a long, coiled tube called your intestines. There, goodness from the food passes into your blood to be carried all round your body.

? *What are teeth for?*

Teeth chomp your food into tiny bits so that it's easier to swallow. Sharp incisors cut it up, pointed canines tear it and big molars at the back crush it.

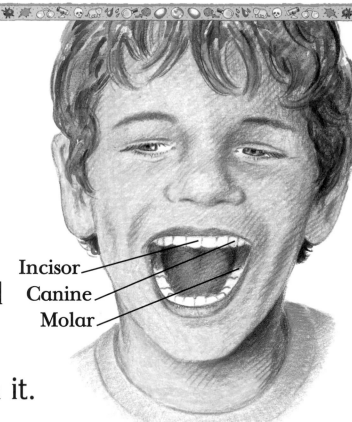

Incisor
Canine
Molar

? *Why do I go to the toilet?*

Your body can't use all the food you eat. The bits you don't need pass out of your body as poo. You also go to the toilet to wee. Wee (or urine) is waste water.

TRUE OR FALSE?

Teeth fall out.

TRUE. Your first 20 teeth, called milk teeth, fall out as bigger adult teeth push up underneath.

Fizzy drinks can make you burp.

TRUE. Fizzy drinks contain lots of bubbles which go into your tummy. Trapped air rushes up from your tummy and you burp!

What's blood for?

Blood carries oxygen and goodness from the food you eat to all the tiny cells in your body to keep them working properly. It travels around your body in narrow tubes called blood vessels.

What does my heart do?

Your heart is a special muscle that keeps working all the time – even when you're fast asleep. Its job is to pump blood all around your body.

From body

To body

To lungs

To lungs

From lungs

Arteries carry blood with oxygen and food to all the parts of your body.

Heart

Veins carry blood without oxygen and food back to your heart.

? *Where's my heart?*

Your heart is right in the middle of your chest, just a little bit to the left, between your lungs. It's about as big as your fist.

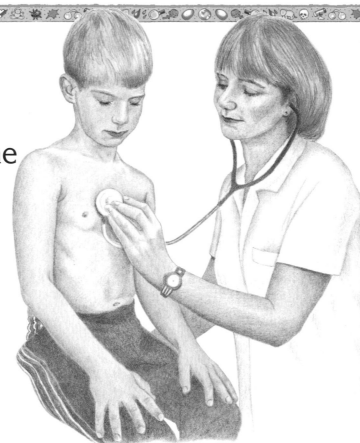

? *Can I feel my heart beating?*

You can sometimes feel your heart beating in your chest if you've been running fast. Or, if you put your fingers on the inside of your wrist, you can feel the throb of your blood moving in time to your heartbeat.

What do my lungs do?

Your lungs take in a gas called oxygen from the air and pass it into your blood. Your blood carries the oxygen from your lungs to the rest of your body. We need oxygen to stay alive. Your lungs are very large. A grown-up's lungs can hold about three litres of air.

What makes me yawn?

You yawn when you haven't been breathing deeply because you're tired or have been sitting still for a long time and you're not getting enough oxygen to your lungs. To take in more oxygen, you suddenly take a big gulp of air through your mouth.

? *What happens when I breathe?*

When you breathe in, your chest expands, your lungs get bigger and air goes up your nose, down your windpipe and into your lungs. When you breathe out, your chest and lungs become smaller and your diaphragm arches upwards to squeeze out stale air. All this happens in just a few seconds.

Windpipe

Lung

Diaphragm

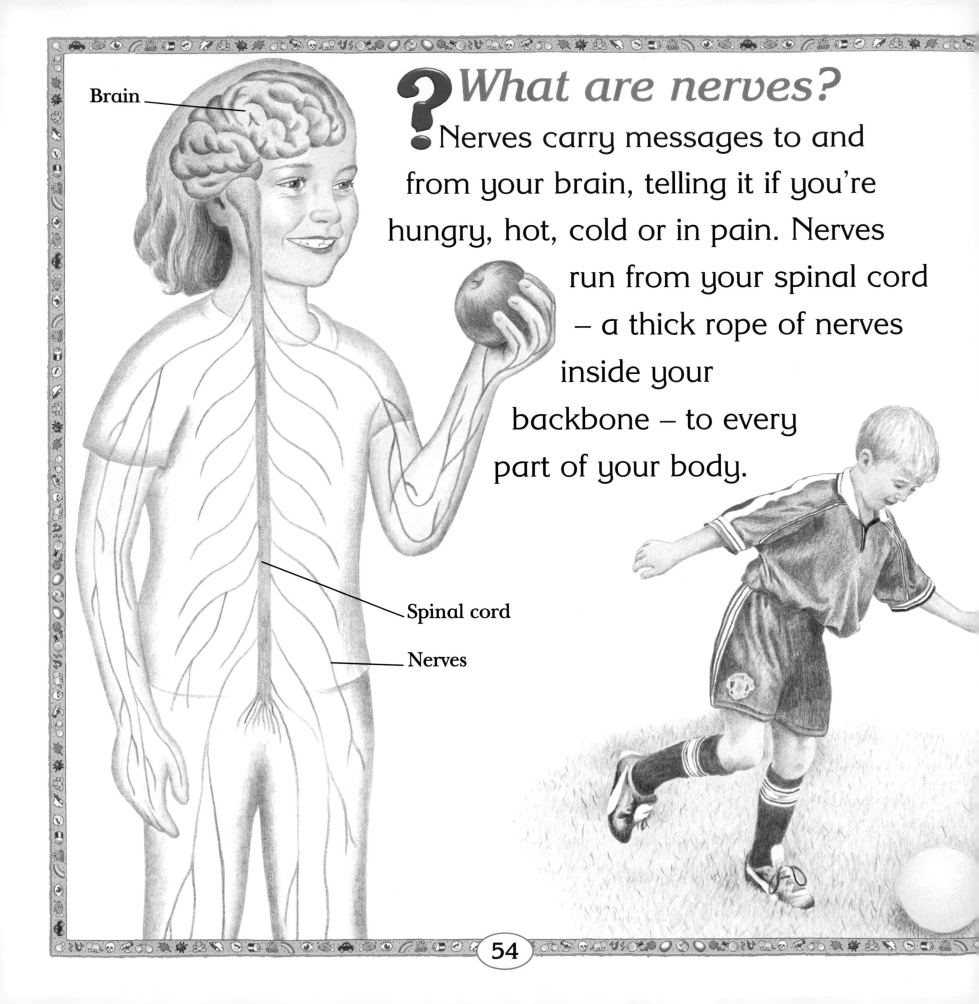

Brain

? What are nerves?

Nerves carry messages to and from your brain, telling it if you're hungry, hot, cold or in pain. Nerves run from your spinal cord – a thick rope of nerves inside your backbone – to every part of your body.

Spinal cord

Nerves

❓ *Why do I get pins and needles?*

If you lie on your arm or leg for a long time, the tiny nerves in them get squashed. When you move again, the nerves may tingle and throb as they start to work again.

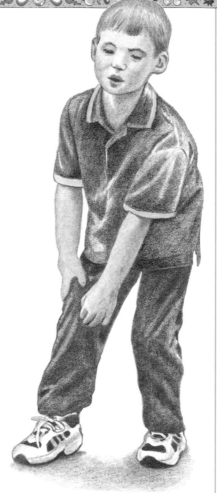

❓ *What does my brain do?*

Your brain sends signals along your nerves telling your body how to work. It stores all your thoughts and memories and controls everything you do.

?How do my eyes help me see?

Each of your eyes is a ball. At the front, there's a black hole called the pupil, which lets in light. Behind the pupil is a lens that helps you to see things close to or far away. The optic nerve carries messages about what you see to your brain.

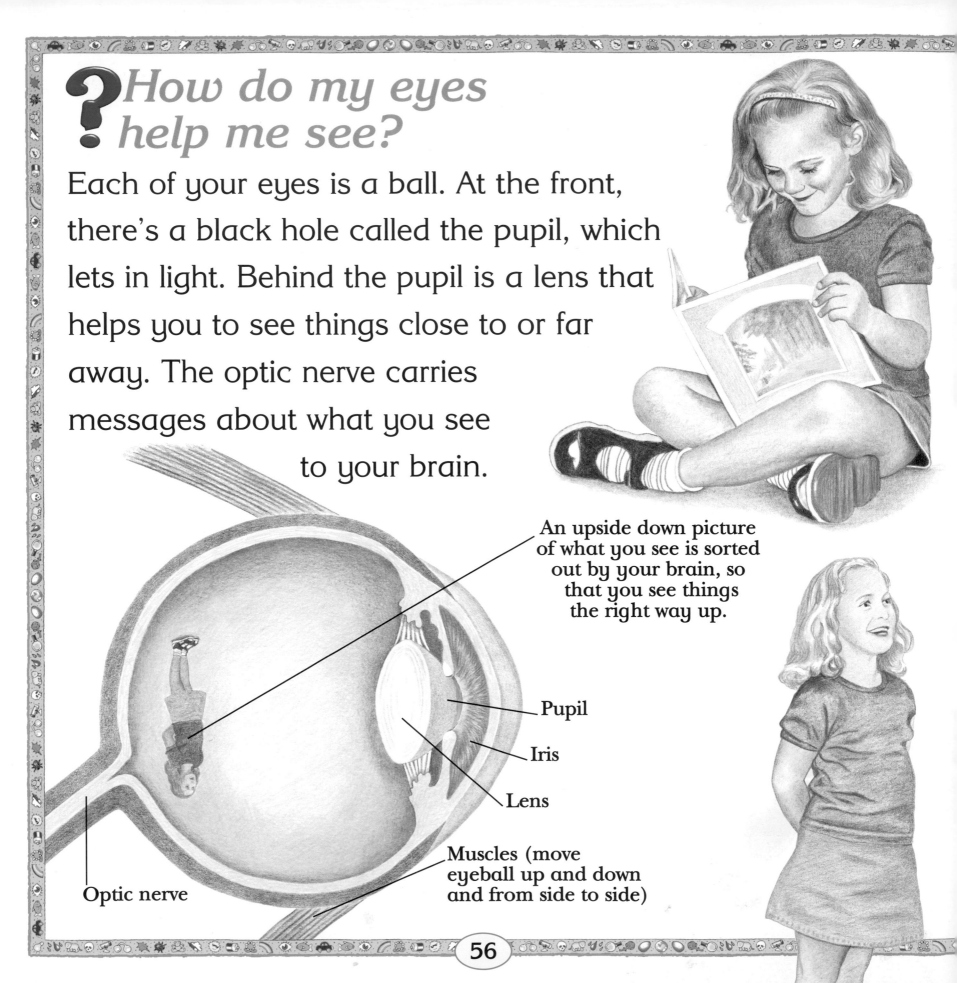

An upside down picture of what you see is sorted out by your brain, so that you see things the right way up.

Pupil

Iris

Lens

Optic nerve

Muscles (move eyeball up and down and from side to side)

? *How do my ears help me hear?*

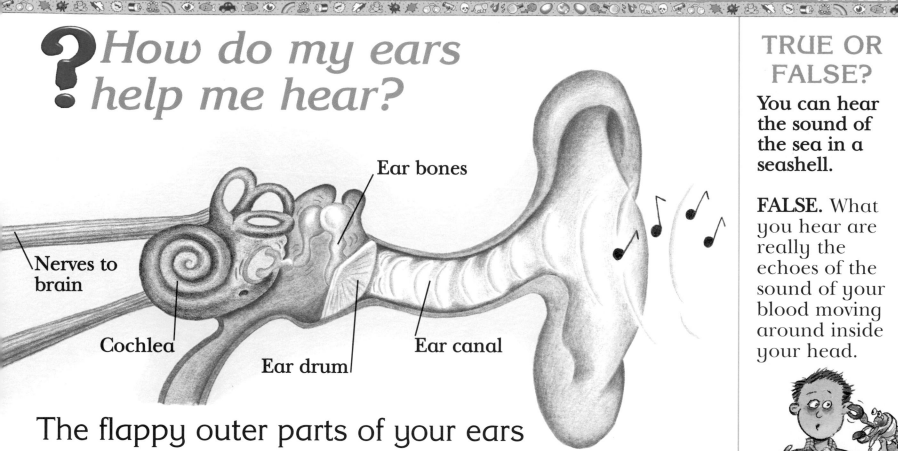

Nerves to brain

Cochlea

Ear drum

Ear bones

Ear canal

The flappy outer parts of your ears collect sounds from the air. The sounds enter your ears as tiny, invisible waves. The waves make your eardrum move up and down, and tiny bones deep inside your ears move, too. Nerves carry sound messages from your ears to your brain.

You can hear the sound of the sea in a seashell.

FALSE. What you hear are really the echoes of the sound of your blood moving around inside your head.

Carrots help you see better.

TRUE. Carrots contain special vitamins that might help you to see a little better in the dark.

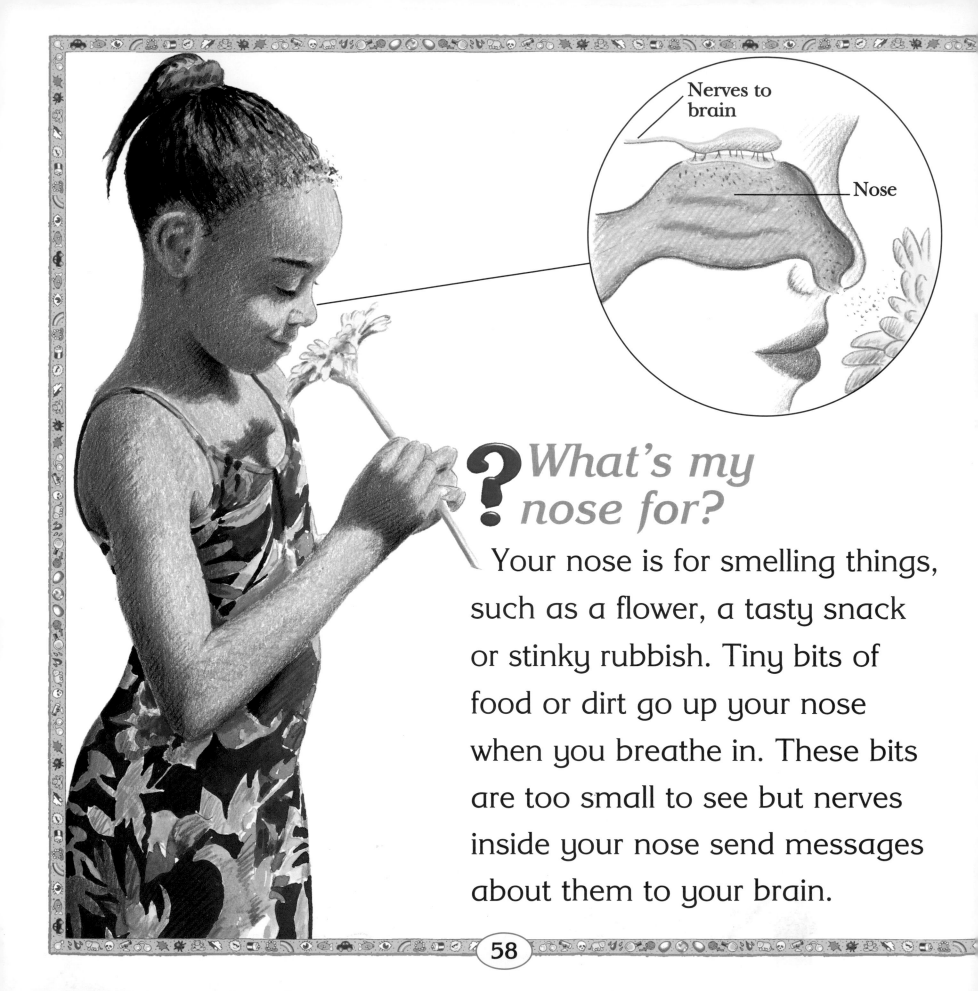

Nerves to brain

Nose

? *What's my nose for?*

Your nose is for smelling things, such as a flower, a tasty snack or stinky rubbish. Tiny bits of food or dirt go up your nose when you breathe in. These bits are too small to see but nerves inside your nose send messages about them to your brain.

? *Why can't I taste food if I have a cold?*

Your sense of smell and taste work together, so if you're eating a crunchy apple, your nose smells how sweet it is and tiny bumps on your tongue (called taste buds) pick up its flavour. When you have a cold, your nose often gets bunged up so it's hard to smell and taste things.

Bitter
Sour
Sweet
Salty

Taste areas of the tongue

? *What is chickenpox?*

Chickenpox is a disease, like mumps and measles. It's quite easy to catch but once you've had it you don't usually get it again. Sometimes, we have injections to stop us catching serious diseases that can make us very ill.

? Why do I sometimes get sick?

You get sick when tiny harmful germs get into your body. Your white blood cells destroy germs by eating them, so that you get better again.

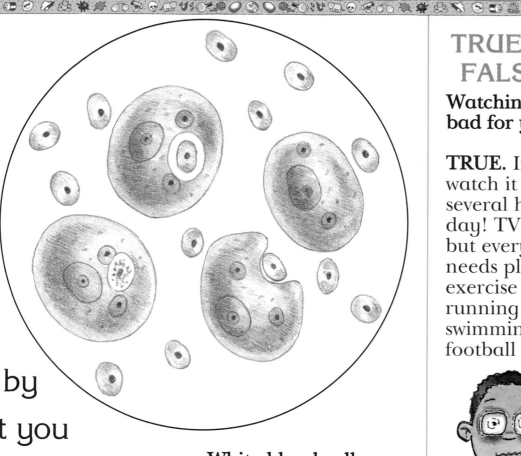

White blood cells eating the invading germs.

? How do I stay healthy?

To stay healthy, you need to eat food that's good for you, drink lots of water, take plenty of exercise and get lots of sleep.

Where did I come from?

You began when a sperm from your father joined with an egg from your mother. A cell formed and began to make more and more cells and a baby – YOU – began to grow. A baby grows inside its mother's womb for nine months.

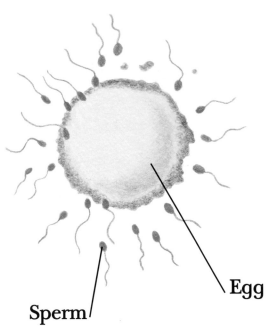

Sperm

Egg

TWO MONTHS

The baby's heart is beating.

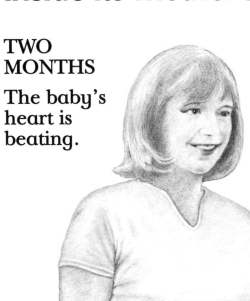

SIX MONTHS

The baby weighs as much as a bag of sugar. It may suck its thumb.

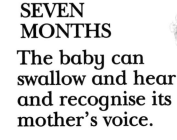

SEVEN MONTHS

The baby can swallow and hear and recognise its mother's voice.

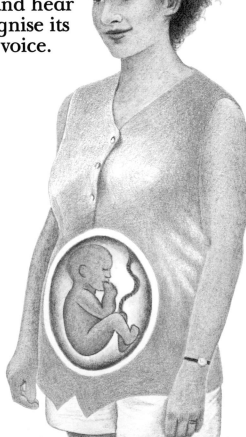

? *What's my tummy button?*

Your tummy button, or your navel, is the place where you were once joined to your mother by a cord called the umbilical cord when you were inside her womb. You got all the food and oxygen you needed to grow through this cord.

NINE MONTHS

At nine months, the baby is plump and strong and nearly ready to be born. It is around 50 cm long and weighs around 3.4 kg.

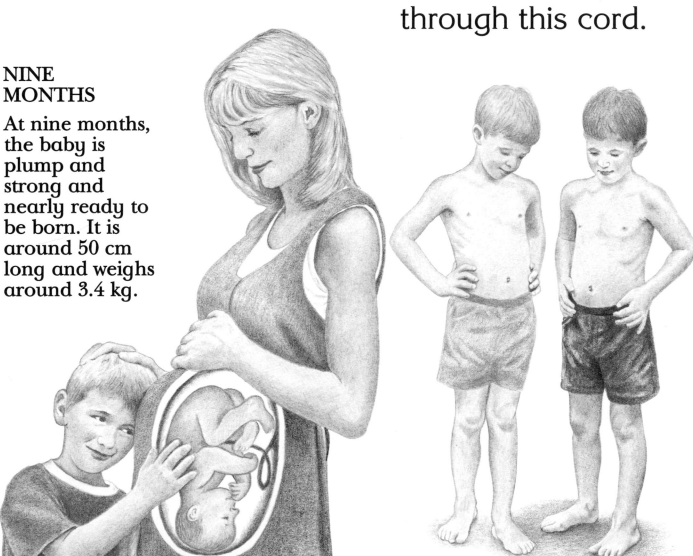

TRUE OR FALSE?

You are still growing.

TRUE. You get taller and stronger and you carry on changing shape, until you're about 18 years old.

Some mothers have more than one baby at a time.

TRUE. Two babies are called twins, four are called quadruplets and six babies are called sextuplets.

? *Why do I sleep?*

You need to sleep to stay healthy. While you're asleep, your body is resting, growing and repairing itself, getting ready for another busy day, and your brain is sorting out your thoughts.

? *Why do I dream?*

Dreams are times during the night when you sleep lightly. Everyone has about five dreams a night but we don't always remember them. Scary dreams are called nightmares. Some are so frightening, they may wake you up.

? *What's sleepwalking?*

Sleepwalking is when someone gets out of bed and walks around when they're still fast asleep. Sleepwalking is quite rare, and no one knows why some people do it.

Which animals have scaly skin?

and other questions about types of animals

What do a mosquito and an elephant have in common?

Although they are very different in shape and size, a mosquito and an elephant have something in common. They are both animals! Animals are living, breathing things that can move around to find food, shelter or a mate.

Sea cucumber

Which plant is really an animal?

Despite their name sea cucumbers are animals, not plants. Their shape and knobbly skin make them look a bit like a cucumber. But unlike cucumber plants, they can move around.

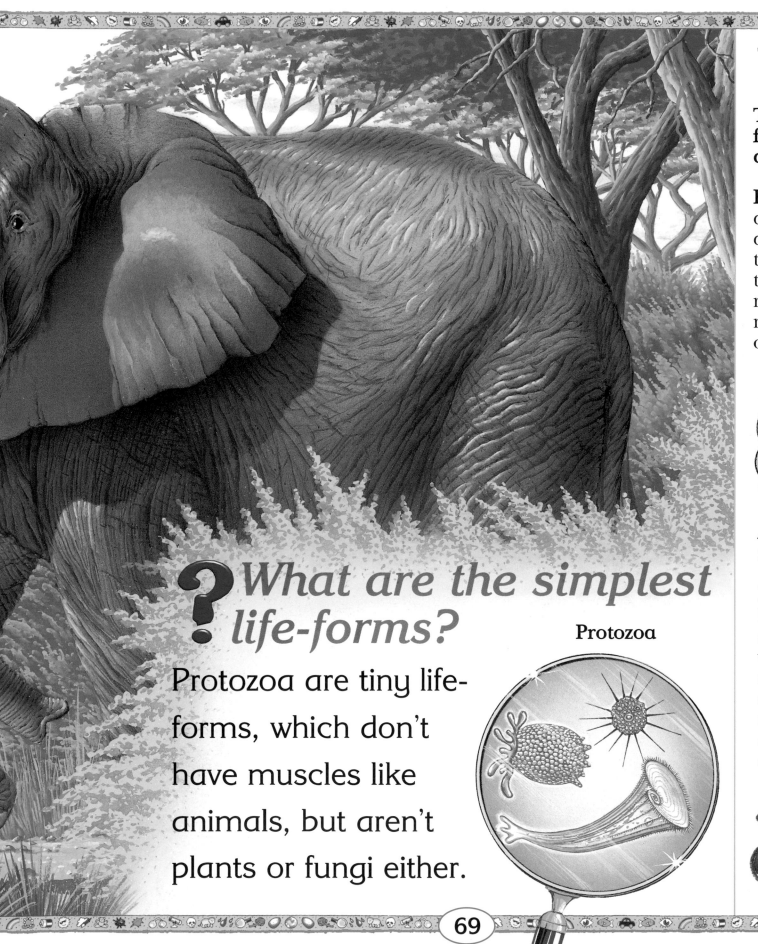

The only life-forms on Earth are animals.

FALSE. Plants and fungi are alive. We know this because they grow and reproduce to make copies of themselves.

All animals need sunshine.

FALSE. At the bottom of the deepest ocean, where it is cold and totally dark, there are tubeworms and other strange creatures.

❓ What are the simplest life-forms?

Protozoa are tiny life-forms, which don't have muscles like animals, but aren't plants or fungi either.

Protozoa

Which animals are spineless?

About 90 per cent of all the animals on Earth have no backbone, or spine. They are called invertebrates and range from snails to big, wobbly jellyfish. All invertebrates are cold-blooded – their body temperature is the same as the air or water around them.

Jellyfish

Giant squid

Which is the biggest boneless creature?

The biggest invertebrate is the giant squid, with an 8 m-long body and even longer tentacles. It lives in the ocean, where the water supports its weight.

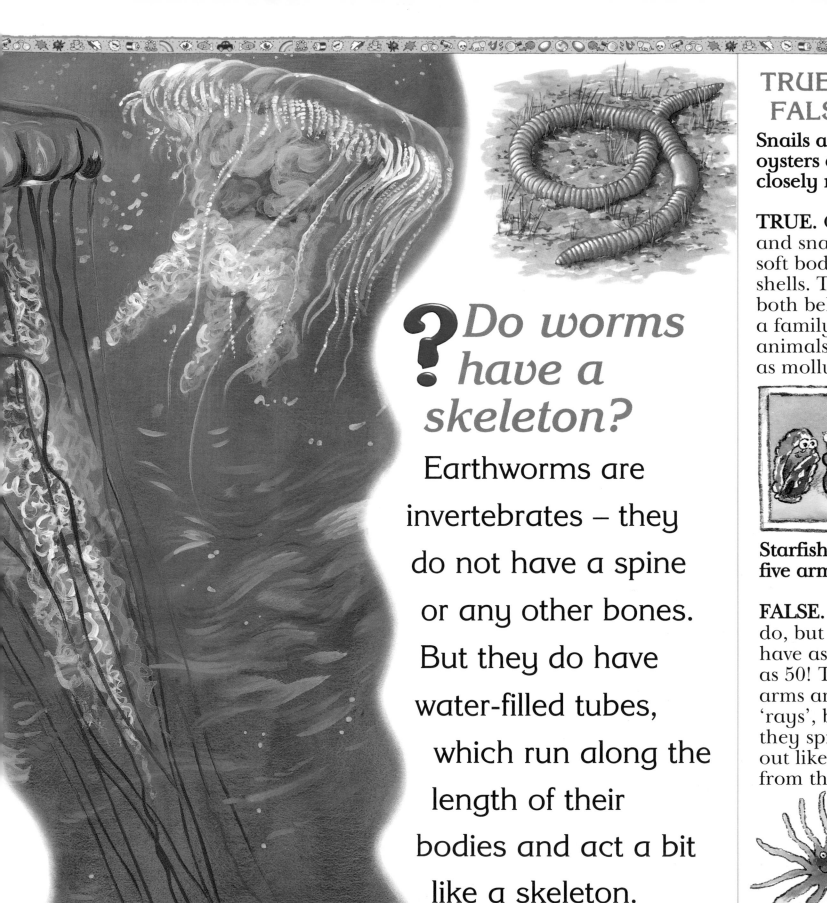

❓ *Do worms have a skeleton?*

Earthworms are invertebrates – they do not have a spine or any other bones. But they do have water-filled tubes, which run along the length of their bodies and act a bit like a skeleton.

TRUE OR FALSE?

Snails and oysters are closely related.

TRUE. Oysters and snails have soft bodies and shells. They both belong to a family of animals known as molluscs.

Starfish have five arms.

FALSE. Most do, but some have as many as 50! The arms are called 'rays', because they spread out like rays from the Sun.

What sort of animal is a lobster?

The lobster is a type of invertebrate called a crustacean. Crustaceans have shells (crusts) and lots of jointed legs. A lobster has five pairs of legs, with claws on its front ones to grip and stab prey.

Who wears armour at the bottom of the sea?

The tough outer shell of a lobster or crab is like a suit of armour, stopping hungry fish and other predators from biting the animal's body. Most crabs live on the seabed, eating rotting remains that sink down there.

Lobster

?How do crabs grow bigger?

Our skin stretches as we grow, but a hard shell can't stretch. When a crab grows too big

Crab losing shell

for its shell, it gets rid of it. The new shell underneath is soft at first, but soon hardens. A crab may do this as many as 20 times in its life.

Stag beetle

? Which animals have a skeleton on the outside?

The tough casing that protects a beetle's body is called an exoskeleton. A crab's shell is a type of exoskeleton, too. Most invertebrates rely on an outside skeleton to protect their boneless body.

? Are spiders insects?

Spiders aren't insects, because they have too many legs and too few body parts! An insect has six legs and three parts to its body (head, thorax and abdomen). A spider has eight legs and its head and thorax are joined.

Tarantula spider

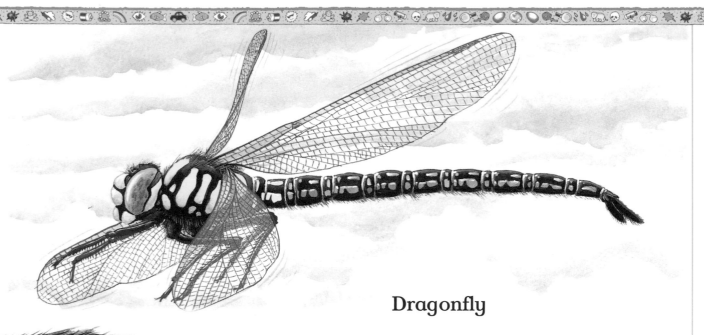

Dragonfly

? Can insects fly?

The ones with wings can! Butterflies, bees and midges are flying insects that have two pairs of wings. Houseflies make do with a single pair. Some insects called termites break off their wings on purpose, when they don't need them anymore.

?How do fish breathe?

Fish have slits called gills on the sides of their heads, that allow them to get oxygen from water, just as we get oxygen from air. All fish breathe using gills.

?How do salmon leap?

Salmon leap if they meet a mini waterfall when they are heading up-river to breed. The strong, muscly tails that they use for swimming also help to thrust them up into the air.

Hammerhead shark

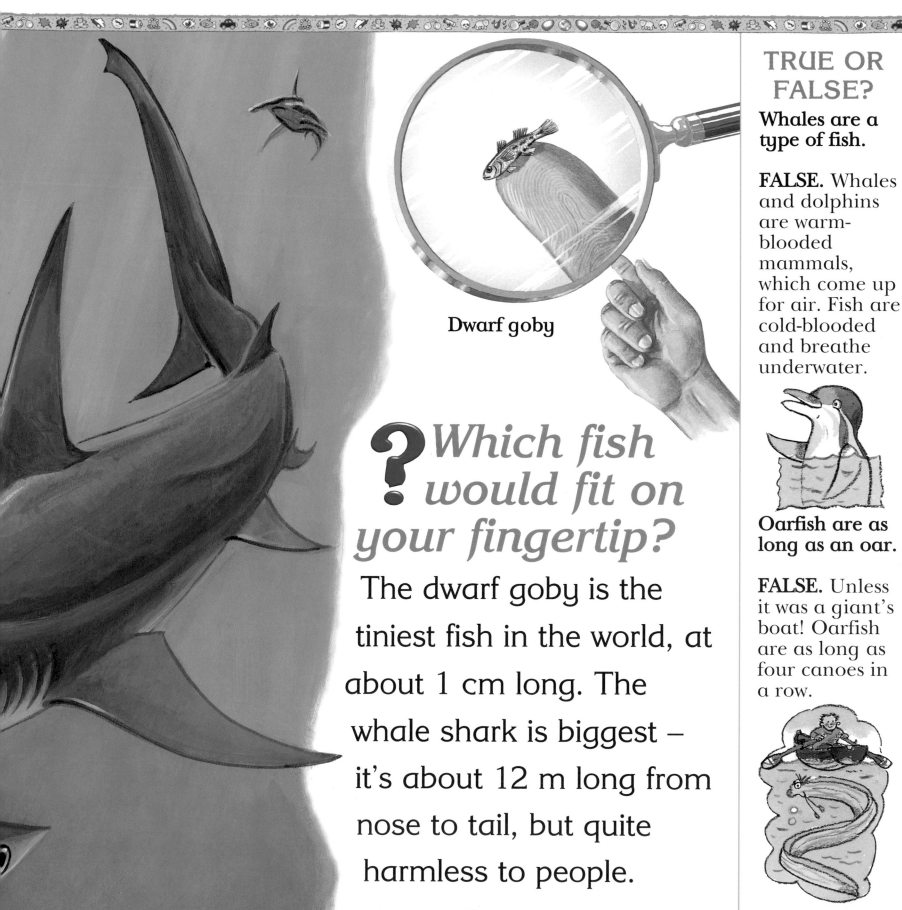

Dwarf goby

? *Which fish would fit on your fingertip?*

The dwarf goby is the tiniest fish in the world, at about 1 cm long. The whale shark is biggest – it's about 12 m long from nose to tail, but quite harmless to people.

? Why are frogs slimy?

A frog's thin, slimy skin allows it to absorb oxygen from both air and water. Frogs are amphibians, animals that start life in water, but gradually change so they can survive on land, too.

Frog

Toad

? How can you tell a frog from a toad?

Most frogs have smooth skin, but toads are warty! Frogs and toads are the only amphibians that lose their tail and grow strong back legs for jumping.

❓ *Which is the weirdest amphibian?*

The axolotl never really grows up! It breeds when it is still at 'tadpole' stage and only changes into an adult body if its pond dries up and it is forced to live on land.

Axolotl

Which animals have scaly skin?

Snakes, lizards, crocodiles and turtles have dry, scaly skin. These cold-blooded creatures belong to a family of animals called reptiles. There are about 6,000 types of reptile.

Tortoise

How long do tortoises live?

Tortoises are the longest-living animals on Earth. Some probably live beyond their 200th birthday! Perhaps it's because their tough, bony shell protects them from dangerous predators.

Alligator

Crocodile

Green python

? *How can you tell a crocodile from an alligator?*

You can tell them apart by their smile. When a crocodile's mouth is shut, you can still see one of its bottom teeth poking out.

❓ *Why do birds have feathers?*

Soft, downy feathers keep birds' bodies toasty and warm, while waxy outer ones keep off the rain. Most importantly, feathers allow birds to fly. Birds beat their feathered wings to lift off the ground and fly through the air.

Parrots

? Can all birds swim?

Penguins

No, but some can. Penguins have webbed feet, stubby wings, oily waterproof feathers, and a layer of fat to keep them warm.

? Why do eagles have such hooked beaks?

Bald eagle

An eagle's hooked beak is perfect for tearing up meat. Herons have long beaks for spearing fish. Macaws have powerful beaks for cracking nuts.

Which animals have fur?

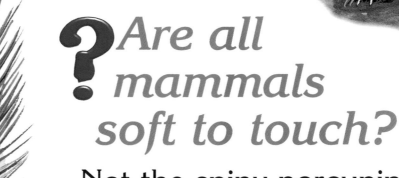

Animals that have fur are called mammals. The other things that mammals have in common are having a backbone, breathing air, being warm-blooded and feeding their babies on milk. The mammal family includes bears and monkeys, bats and mice.

Are all mammals soft to touch?

Not the spiny porcupine! Although it is related to rats and mice and does have fur, the porcupine also has lots of spiky quills to protect it from its enemies.

Porcupine

Bumblebee bat

? **Which is the tiniest mammal?**

The smallest mammal is the bumblebee bat that lives in caves in Thailand. The bat's body is only about 3 cm long. Its wingspan is much longer – about 14 cm!

TRUE OR FALSE?

All mammals live on land.

FALSE. Manatees, seals and whales live in water. They have flippers and tails, not arms and legs.

Humans are mammals.

TRUE. Hair is a type of fur, and we feed our babies on milk. Humans are primates, like chimps and gorillas.

❓ What type of animal is a koala?

Along with kangaroos, koalas belong to a group of mammals called marsupials. Tiny baby koalas live in their mother's pouch, where they can feed on her milk for the first seven months of their life.

Koala and young

❓ Which mammal lays eggs?

Duckbilled platypus

Unlike most mammals, the duckbilled platypus lays eggs that hatch after about ten days. The mother feeds her babies on milk, until they are big enough to hunt for fish.

Humpback whale

❓ Do all mammals breathe through the mouth?

No – whales breathe through a blowhole on the top of their head. When they surface, warm breath pushes out. Out in the cold, it makes a misty spout that can be as high as 12 m!

Which lizard looks like a tree trunk?

The leaf-tailed gecko's speckled skin blends in perfectly with the trunk of a tree. So long as this reptile keeps still, its clever camouflage stops any predator from noticing it.

Gecko

Zebras

Why are zebras stripy?

Black and white stripes confuse lions and other predators. The stripes seem to wobble in the heat haze. Each zebra has its own pattern, so stripes might also help foals find their mum in the herd.

? *Who wears two fur coats?*

Some mammals change their coat to match the season, including the hares, foxes and wolves of the snowy north. Their brown coat turns white in winter for camouflage against the snow. It also grows extra-thick to keep out the cold.

Arctic fox

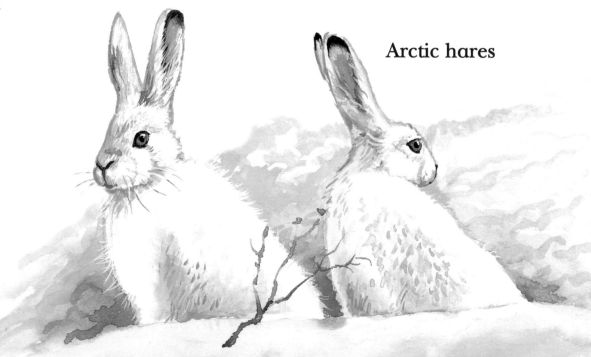

Arctic hares

Ostrich

❓ Do turtles lay eggs in the sea?

Turtles spend all their lives out at sea, but the mums come ashore to lay their leathery eggs. When the eggs hatch, the baby turtles crawl out of the sand and head straight down to the water.

❓ Which bird lays the biggest egg?

The biggest bird lays the biggest egg! An ostrich is much taller than an adult human, and its eggs are giant, too. A single ostrich egg weighs more than 22 chicken eggs!

❓ *Do tree frogs lay eggs in trees?*

Like all frogs, tiny tree frogs need to lay their eggs in water. They use pools of rainwater cupped in the leaves of rainforest trees. There's fresh rain every day, so there's little danger of the eggs drying out.

Tree frog

Baby turtles

Seahorse

? Which dad has babies?

After seahorses mate, the male carries the eggs in a pouch. When it's time for the eggs to hatch, hundreds of tiny seahorses squirt out! Seahorses get their name because their head looks a bit like a horse's – but really they are fish! They have fins and a tail, and they breathe through gills.

? *Which baby bounces along?*

A baby kangaroo, or joey, has a very bouncy ride in its mum's pouch as she hops around. The joey is only about 2 cm long when it is born. It crawls up through its mum's fur into her pouch and stays there, drinking her milk. The joey only leaves the cosy pouch when it is about nine months old.

Kangaroo

How well do sharks smell?

Sharks smell very well! As a shark swims, water flows in and out of its nose. If the shark picks up the scent of blood it makes a beeline for it, 'sniffing' hard to stay on course.

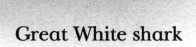

Great White shark

Hares

Why do rabbits have big ears?

Rabbits and hares have enormous ears for their size – and super hearing. The twitchy, outsize ears funnel the sound. Big ears also allow heat to escape, so the animals stay cool.

❓ How do eagles find their prey?

By sight – like all birds of prey, eagles have keen eyesight. A golden eagle can spot a rabbit's slightest movement on the ground from 2 km away!

Golden eagle

Why are jungles in danger?

and other questions about things that grow

Where do plants live?

Plants live everywhere! They grow in towns and cities, in the countryside, in streams, lakes and rivers, and by the sea. Some plants can live where we cannot. Cacti survive in hot, dry deserts, and some tiny flowering plants live at the top of freezing cold mountains.

? *How many kinds of plants are there?*

There are around 400,000 different kinds of plants. They come in all sorts of shapes and sizes from tiny lichens that grow on rocks, beautiful flowers, and towering trees that reach towards the sky.

TRUE OR FALSE?

Plants live in the sea.

TRUE. Marine, or sea, plants include lots of different kinds of seaweed, such as kelp and sea lettuce.

Trees are the biggest plants.

TRUE. Coast redwood trees in California, USA, are the tallest plants in the world. They can grow more than 100 m high.

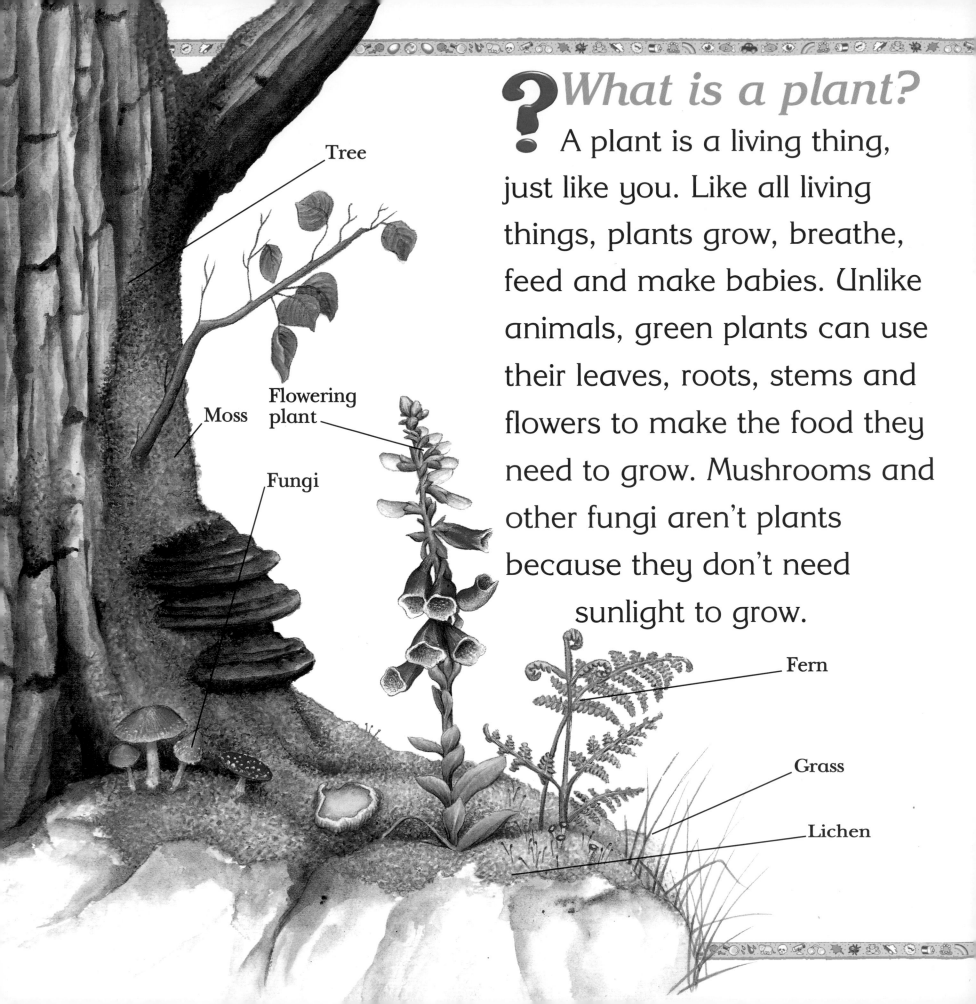

❓ *What is a plant?*

A plant is a living thing, just like you. Like all living things, plants grow, breathe, feed and make babies. Unlike animals, green plants can use their leaves, roots, stems and flowers to make the food they need to grow. Mushrooms and other fungi aren't plants because they don't need sunlight to grow.

Tree

Moss

Flowering plant

Fungi

Fern

Grass

Lichen

❓ *Why do plants have roots?*

A plant needs roots to hold it in the soil so that it doesn't blow over in the wind. Tall trees need longer, stronger roots than small flowering plants. Roots also suck up water from the soil and carry it up the trunk or stem to the rest of the plant.

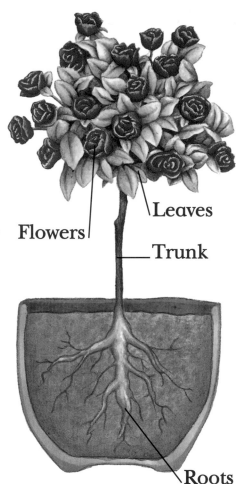

Flowers

Leaves

Trunk

Roots

❓ *What do plants need to grow?*

Plants need sunlight, water, air and space to grow. Most plants will die if they are left in the dark or uprooted from damp soil.

TRUE OR FALSE?

Every plant has roots in the soil.

FALSE. Some plants grow on other plants, not in the soil. These plants are called epiphytes. They include beautiful orchid flowers.

Plants are able to move.

TRUE. Plants don't walk or run but they do move as they grow. Some climbing plants twist around other plants as they grow upwards.

? *Why do plants have leaves?*

Because leaves work hard, making food for the plant to grow. Green leaves contain a green colouring called chlorophyll. The chlorophyll uses sunlight and a gas from the air, called carbon dioxide, to change water into a kind of sugar. The sugar feeds the plant. This way of making food is called photosynthesis.

Sunlight

Food to roots

Oxygen

Carbon Dioxide

❓ Why do some leaves change colour in the autumn?

Green leaves change colour when their green colouring, or chlorophyll, breaks down. Other colours then show through and the leaves look brown, red or yellowy gold.

❓ Why do plants have stems?

Stems grow towards the sunlight and support the plants' leaves, so that they can make food. Stems also carry water, minerals and sugary food (called sap) around the plant. Some plants have straight stems, others are curly.

Sweet pea

Sunflower stem

TRUE OR FALSE?

All trees have leaves.

FALSE. The saguaro cactus is a leafless tree. Instead of leaves, it has chlorophyll in its thick, green stems, which make food and store water.

Plants sweat.

TRUE. During photosynthesis, plants give off water. Just look at the water on the windows of a greenhouse!

❓ *Why do trees lose their leaves?*

Some trees lose their leaves in the wintertime when there is less sunlight and water freezes in the ground. These trees, called deciduous trees, rest during the winter. They store enough food during the summer to keep themselves alive until the following spring when new leaves grow.

? What are growing rings?

A growing ring is added to a tree's trunk every year. The ring is thick if the tree has grown a lot during a warm, long summer with plenty of rain, and thin if the tree has not grown much because the weather has been harsh.

Bark

Growing rings

? Do all trees lose their leaves?

No – some trees keep their leaves all year round. They are called evergreens because they are always, or forever, green. They include spruces and pine trees.

TRUE OR FALSE?

Plants sleep.

TRUE. Green plants can only make food during the day when there's lots of sunlight. At night, they shut down and have a rest.

Some trees are ancient.

TRUE. The giant sequoia can live for over 2,000 years. Some bristlecone pines are over 4,500 years old! They're the world's oldest trees.

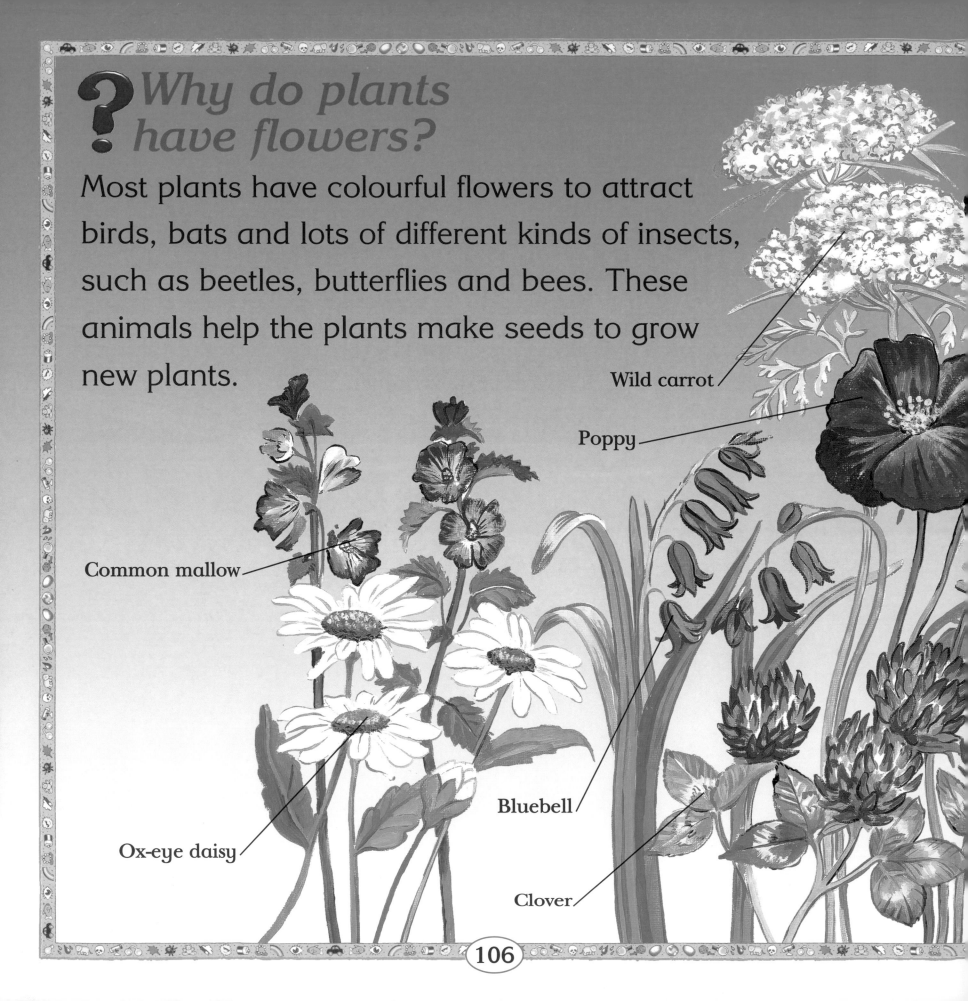

Why do plants have flowers?

Most plants have colourful flowers to attract birds, bats and lots of different kinds of insects, such as beetles, butterflies and bees. These animals help the plants make seeds to grow new plants.

Wild carrot

Poppy

Common mallow

Bluebell

Ox-eye daisy

Clover

?Why do flowers smell?

Sweet-smelling flowers help to attract animals. The scent tells insects and other animals that the flower contains a sweet, sugary juice called nectar which the animals like to drink.

?How are seeds made?

Flowers have male parts called stamens and female parts called carpels. The stamens make tiny grains of pollen. The carpels contain eggs, called ovules. Seeds are made when the pollen reaches the ovules. This is called pollination.

All flowers smell sweet.

FALSE. The rafflesia plant smells like rotten meat! This attracts flies that like pongy smells.

Some flowers open at night.

TRUE. The evening primrose opens its petals at night and lets out a sweet scent to attract night-flying moths.

❓ *How do insects help flowers?*

Insects help to pollinate flowers by carrying pollen from the carpels of one flower to the ovules of another flower. When a bee feeds on the sweet nectar in a flower, pollen sticks to the bee's furry body. The pollen brushes off on to the next flower visited by the bee.

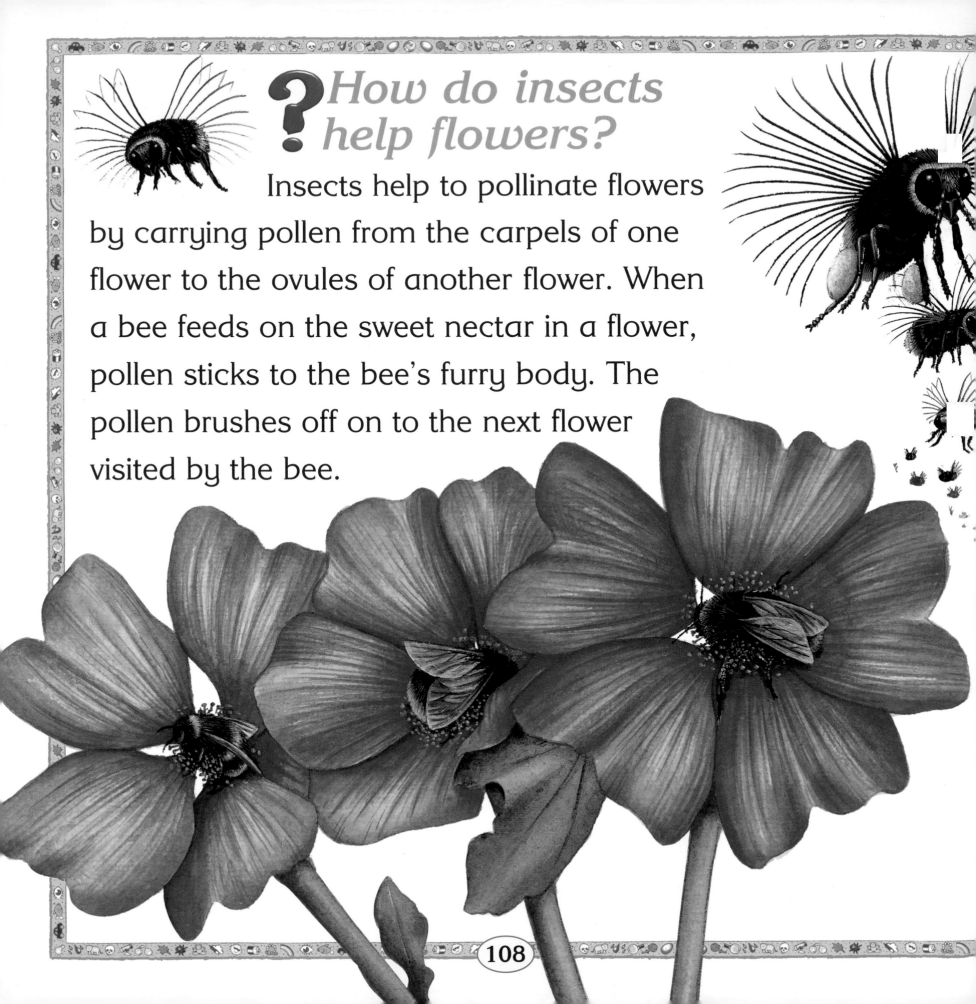

? Why do some birds drink from flowers?

Some birds like to drink nectar, too. The hummingbird sucks up nectar through its long straw-like beak. As it feeds, its head brushes against the flower's pollen grains.

? Which flowers do bats like?

Some bats like to feed on the bird of paradise flower. The part of the plant that makes pollen is flat for the bat to perch on.

Pollen is tiny.

TRUE. Pollen grains are so small that 50 or so would fit on the head of a pin!

All plants need animals for pollination.

FALSE. Some plants, such as goosegrass, pollinate themselves. Sometimes the wind blows dry pollen on to the female parts of nearby plants. This happens with most grasses and trees.

❓How many seeds are in each fruit?

Some fruits, such as peaches, mangoes and avocadoes, contain just one large seed inside a hard stone. Other fruits, such as oranges, lemons, apples and pears, contain several seeds called pips. Berries have lots of tiny pips around the outside of each fruit.

?How do plants look after their seeds?

Many seeds have hard coats or cases to protect them as they grow. Some plants also have tasty, colourful fruits growing around their seeds. Animals eat the seeds along with the fruit. This helps to spread the seeds.

Inside an avocado

Skin

Flesh

Seed

Hard seed coating

Which seeds can fly?

Some small, light seeds float in the air. Sycamore seeds have wings. Dandelion seeds have tiny parachutes. Other seeds are round and heavy so that they drop to the ground and roll away from their parent to get enough space to grow.

Dandelion seed

Lime seed

Sycamore seed

? *How do animals help to spread seeds?*

When animals eat fruit they may spit out the seeds or the seeds pass through the animal and fall to the ground as droppings. Sometimes seeds with tiny hooks or spines stick to an animal's fur and are carried a long way before they fall.

❓ *What do seeds need?*

Like large plants, seeds need light, air, water and space to grow. Seeds mostly grow in spring, when the soil warms in the sun and there is plenty of rain. Some seeds are planted on purpose by people to grow flowers, fruit and vegetables.

How do seeds grow?

The seed swells up in damp soil until its seed case bursts. A tiny root then pushes down into the soil and a thin shoot pushes up towards the light. When a seed starts to grow, we say it germinates.

Avocado

Carrot tops

Beans

Mustard and cress

Which plants are fun to grow?

Marigolds, nasturtiums, peas, beansprouts and mustard and cress are all easy and fun to grow from seeds. You can even grow a plant from a carrot top!

Roots grow from seeds first of all.

TRUE. Roots grow first to take in water from the soil. Shoots and stems then grow from the other end of the seed.

Seeds need to grow quickly.

FALSE. Some seeds that grow in the desert can wait years for the rains to come before they can grow.

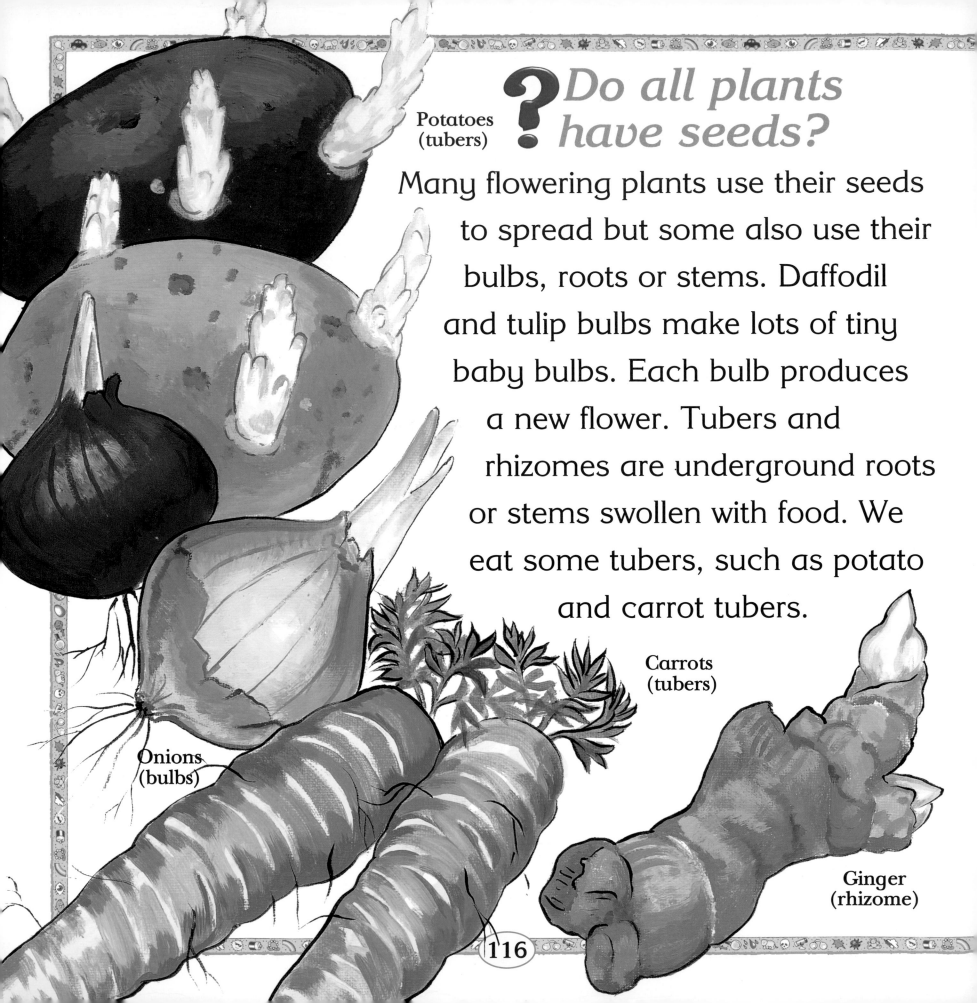

Potatoes (tubers)

❓ Do all plants have seeds?

Many flowering plants use their seeds to spread but some also use their bulbs, roots or stems. Daffodil and tulip bulbs make lots of tiny baby bulbs. Each bulb produces a new flower. Tubers and rhizomes are underground roots or stems swollen with food. We eat some tubers, such as potato and carrot tubers.

Carrots (tubers)

Onions (bulbs)

Ginger (rhizome)

? *Which plants have runners?*

Plants such as wild strawberries have long stems called runners that stretch down into the soil. New roots and shoots grow from each runner then the runner rots away.

Strawberry plant

Runner

? *What are spores?*

Spores are tiny, dust-like specks made by lichens, mosses or ferns. These plants don't have flowers or seeds. Instead, the spores fly away to make new plants.

Spores

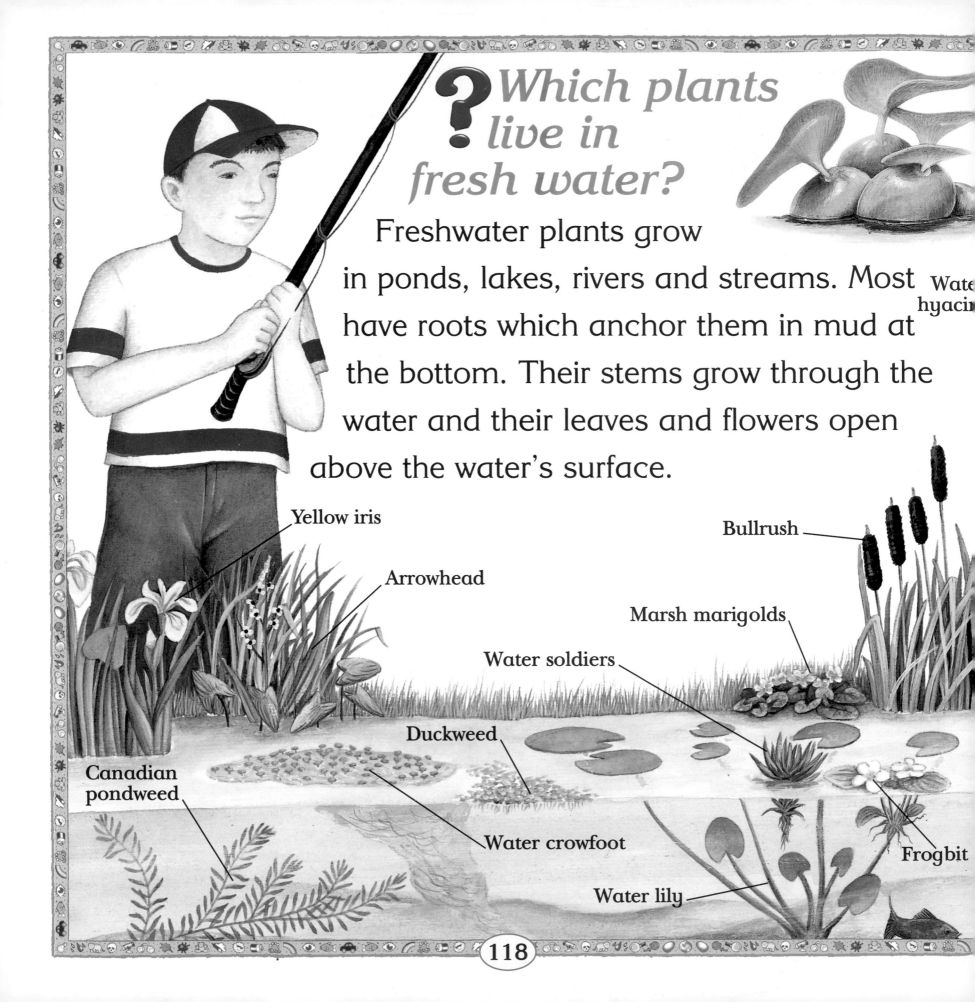

❓Which plants live in fresh water?

Freshwater plants grow in ponds, lakes, rivers and streams. Most have roots which anchor them in mud at the bottom. Their stems grow through the water and their leaves and flowers open above the water's surface.

Water hyaci...

Yellow iris

Arrowhead

Bullrush

Marsh marigolds

Water soldiers

Duckweed

Canadian pondweed

Water crowfoot

Water lily

Frogbit

Seaweeds do not have roots. Instead they fasten on to rocks using a structure called a holdfast.

? *Which plants live in sea water?*

Seaweed is a kind of plant called alga that lives in salty water. Algae can be red, brown, green or blue but they still contain chlorophyll for making food from sunlight. Some seaweeds fasten themselves on to rocks. Others have bubbles of air in their leaves so they can float.

Channelled wrack

Bladder wrack

Red seaweed
Sea lettuce

TRUE OR FALSE?

Water plants often have two kinds of leaves.

TRUE. Leaves below the water are often small to avoid water damage. Leaves above are larger, to catch the light.

Seaweed can grow as tall as trees.

TRUE. Kelp can grow up to 200 metres long! Forests of kelp grow near California.

Are some plants dangerous?

Some plants are poisonous to stop animals eating them. Poisonous plants include foxgloves, lupins, deadly nightshade and belladonna. Poison ivy may leave blisters if it touches bare skin. Nettles have tiny hairs on their leaves that inject you with poison if you brush against them.

Rose

Cactus

Which plants have weapons?

Brambles and roses have thorns, cacti have sharp spines and holly has spiky leaves, to stop animals eating them.

Holly

? *Which plants eat meat?*

Some plants eat insects as well as making their own food. When an insect touches a delicate hair on the inside of the leaves of a Venus flytrap, the leaves snap shut, trapping the insect inside. Insects landing on the edge of the pitcher plant slip into a pool of liquid at the bottom and drown.

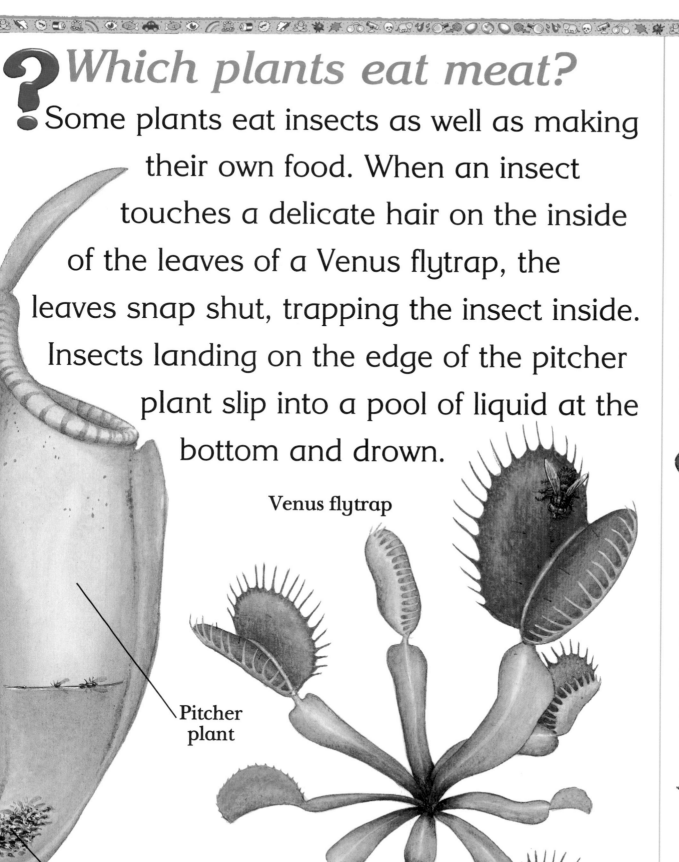

Pitcher plant

Insect soup

Venus flytrap

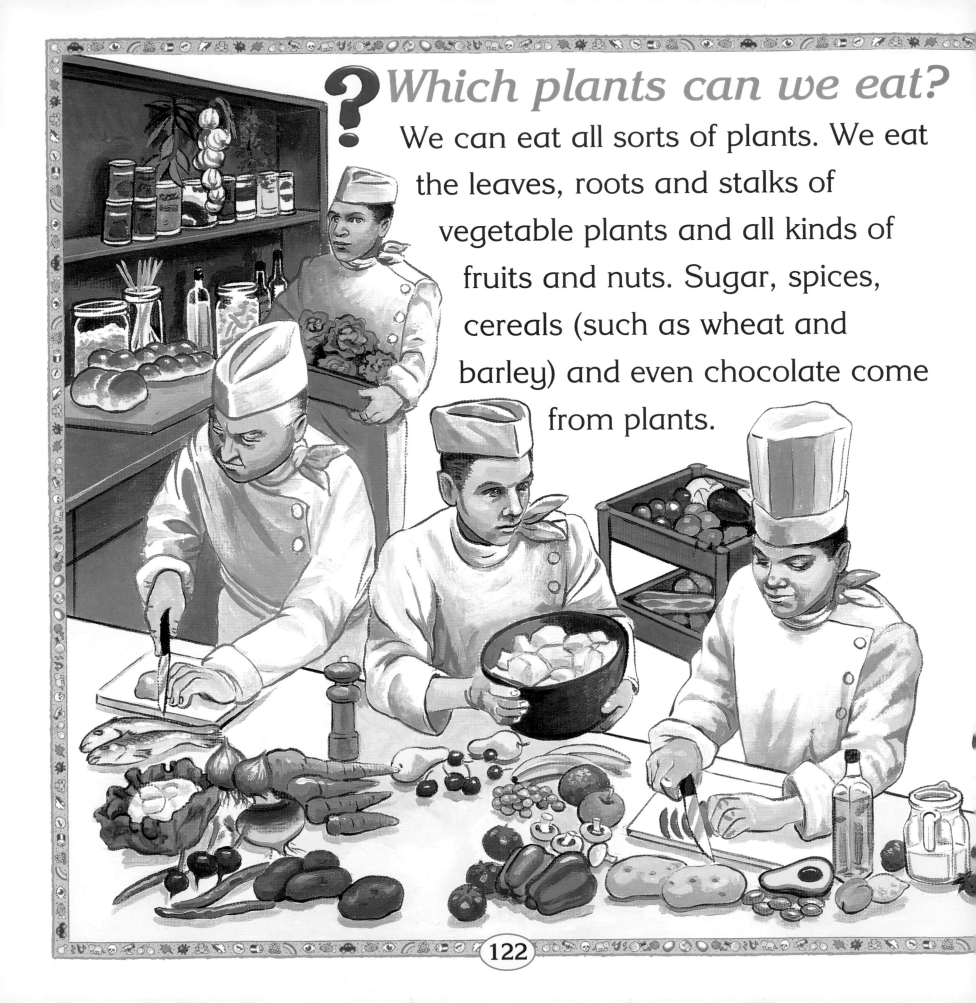

Which plants can we eat?

We can eat all sorts of plants. We eat the leaves, roots and stalks of vegetable plants and all kinds of fruits and nuts. Sugar, spices, cereals (such as wheat and barley) and even chocolate come from plants.

How do plants help us?

Plants give us lots of other things as well as food. Cotton cloth comes from the cotton plant and linen comes from a plant called flax. Plants are also used to make oil, beauty products and medicines.

Eucalyptus
(cold cures)

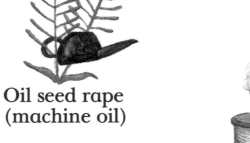

Oil seed rape
(machine oil)

Cotton
(clothes)

Aloe vera
(face creams)

Seaweed
(photographic film)

Foxglove
(heart medicine)

TRUE OR FALSE?

Plants give us good ideas.

TRUE. The burdock plant has tiny hooked spines. It gave us the idea for Velcro fasteners on clothes, shoes and bags.

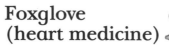

This book was really made from plants.

TRUE. Books are made from paper. Most paper comes from trees.

Are plants in danger?

Plants are in danger from forest fires, pollution from car exhaust fumes and smoking factory chimneys. Building new homes and roads is also dangerous for the places where many plants live and grow.

Why are jungles in danger?

Jungles are in danger of being destroyed forever because so many trees are being cut down for wood or to clear land for farming. When this happens, many kinds of plants and animals may die out.

? *Can I help to protect plants?*

Yes – don't pick wild flowers, especially in nature reserves. Try to grow a tree in your garden or in a park, or sow your own wild garden from seeds.

Trees grow again if they are cut down.

TRUE. But very slowly. It takes hundreds of years for a whole forest to regrow. More than 400 types of plant die out every year.

Plants harm other plants.

TRUE. The strangler fig winds around a tree as it grows, until eventually the tree dies.

Index